"We live in an extremely politicized and polarized age with many big personalities out in front. But this isn't exactly a new phenomenon. Tim Cooper's wonderful little book gives us realistic historical reflections that then generate relevant practical advice for us. He encourages us to look back in order that we might learn from (flawed) heroes of the past even as we seek to navigate our own (flawed) engagement in the present. This is a genuinely helpful volume."

Kelly M. Kapic, Professor of Theological Studies, Covenant College; author, *You're Only Human*

"In *When Christians Disagree*, Tim Cooper investigates the impact of personality and pride, history and hostility, and experience and environment on the tragic breakdown of peace between two giants of the Puritan movement—John Owen and Richard Baxter. Demonstrating that every believer (and pastor) has blind spots, struggles with sin, and wrestles with pride, Cooper draws practical implications for Christians striving to cultivate unity and humility in the body of Christ. The reflections of this insightful, balanced, and accessible work are invaluable for pastoral ministry, historical analysis, and practical Christian living. Above all, the failures that Cooper highlights in the lives of Owen and Baxter should encourage us to boast alone in the one perfect man—the spotless Lamb of God whose glories these men rejoiced to proclaim."

Joel R. Beeke, Chancellor and Professor of Homiletics and Systematic Theology, Puritan Reformed Theological Seminary

"In an age of increasing tribalism, this little book gives us an important lesson in wisdom. While well written, it is a painful read, for as Cooper describes it, it is like watching a car crash in slow motion to see the clash between Baxter and Owen, two godly but human giants of seventeenth-century English Christianity. There is much here for us to learn: the complexity of factors, prejudices, and (potentially distorting) filters that make for disagreements between Christians. May God use this volume to increase our humility and our prudence as we navigate disagreements today and strive for healthy unity in the gospel."

Michael Reeves, President and Professor of Theology, Union School of Theology, United Kingdom

"Disagreements in the family of God are rarely dispassionate affairs because they are born out of the most deeply held convictions of complex creatures. Tim Cooper masterfully illustrates this dynamic in his account of the tragic feud between John Owen and Richard Baxter. This volume represents the best kind of church history—personal, probing, and directly applicable to contemporary Christian life."

Rhyne R. Putman, Vice President of Academic Affairs, Williams Baptist University; Professor of Theology and Culture, New Orleans Baptist Theological Seminary; author, *When Doctrine Divides the People of God*

When Christians Disagree

When Christians Disagree

*Lessons from the Fractured Relationship of
John Owen and Richard Baxter*

Tim Cooper

Foreword by Michael A. G. Haykin

WHEATON, ILLINOIS

When Christians Disagree: Lessons from the Fractured Relationship of John Owen and Richard Baxter

© 2024 by Tim Cooper

Published by Crossway
        1300 Crescent Street
        Wheaton, Illinois 60187

First printing 2024

Printed in the United States of America

Trade paperback ISBN: 978-1-4335-9295-9
ePub ISBN: 978-1-4335-9296-6
PDF ISBN: 978-1-4335-9297-3

Library of Congress Cataloging-in-Publication Data

Names: Cooper, Tim, 1970– author.
Title: When Christians disagree : lessons from the fractured relationship of John Owen and Richard Baxter / Tim Cooper ; foreword by Michael Haykin.
Description: Wheaton, Illinois : Crossway, 2024. | Includes bibliographical references and index.
Identifiers: LCCN 2023032991 (print) | LCCN 2023032992 (ebook) | ISBN 9781433592959 (trade paperback) | ISBN 9781433592973 (pdf) | ISBN 9781433592966 (epub)
Subjects: LCSH: Puritans—England—History. | Owen, John, 1616–1683. | Baxter, Richard, 1615–1691. | Polarization (Social Sciences)—Religious aspects—Christianity—History.
Classification: LCC BX9334.3 .C67 2024 (print) | LCC BX9334.3 (ebook) | DDC 285/.9092242—dc23/eng/20240222
LC record available at https://lccn.loc.gov/2023032991
LC ebook record available at https://lccn.loc.gov/2023032992

Crossway is a publishing ministry of Good News Publishers.

VP   33   32   31   30   29   28   27   26   25   24
15   14   13   12   11   10   9   8   7   6   5   4   3   2   1

Contents

Foreword

TEACHING AND READING about the history of Christianity inevitably entails significant consideration of the controversies that have divided men and women in the church: from serious conflicts such as those about Arianism and Pelagianism in the ancient church to divisions over secondary matters like the nature of church governance, baptism, and the gifts of the Spirit in more recent times. One way of reflecting on such conflicts, often found in handbooks of historical theology, has been to see such controversies as fundamentally doctrinal in origin. With the rise of social history in the past half century or so, socioeconomic factors have also been brought to bear on the explanation of these theological disputes. Both of these ways of understanding ecclesial conflict in the past—and present—are helpful. Given the complexity of human life and the human person, however, we must invariably take other, more personal factors into consideration.

In this exceptional study of the relationship of John Owen and Richard Baxter—chief among the leaders of later seventeenth-century Puritanism—such personal factors are key to understanding why they failed to work together in the face of a hostile state church. Of course, neither of them could admit that their differences were not simply theological. But Tim Cooper shows that there was more going on in their relationship than a failure to agree on how to read and exegete the Scriptures. In doing so, he demonstrates that church history is about more than theology and biblical reflection. It involves human personalities and their deepest affections. And the failure of Owen and Baxter to get along to some degree as fellow pilgrims to the same heavenly city had dire effects for the earthly fortunes of their respective ecclesial communities.

This is a must-read for anyone who wishes to understand something of why and how Christians can fail to live up to their calling to be men and women brimful with the fruit of the Spirit. May we, in this day when Christians must be all that Christ calls us to be, learn from the failure of our older brothers in the faith.

Michael A. G. Haykin
THE SOUTHERN BAPTIST THEOLOGICAL SEMINARY
LOUISVILLE, KENTUCKY

Introduction

NOT LONG AGO I was driving to my local supermarket when I noticed a sequence of small billboards that encouraged people to moderate the force of their online disagreements. "Tone it down," urged one message. "There is more that unites us than divides us," observed another. There can be no doubting the need for those encouragements. We seem to live in a world of increasing polarization in which the members of warring tribes address each other with remarkable vitriol in the online environment, and our disagreements show no sign of narrowing. Technology has played a large part in that development, not least the rapid emergence of social media platforms in which people use words and sentiments they would much less likely deploy if they were speaking to the other person face-to-face. We do indeed need to tone it down before our differences become unbridgeable.

So I was struck by the relevance of that billboard campaign for our current cultural, societal, and political moment. More than that, I was struck by how precisely pertinent those sentiments are to a much older story, one that unfolded nearly four centuries ago. They apply now; they applied back then. That was a world away from the omnipresent social media we now experience, but those who lived in seventeenth-century England were coming to grips with the rapid proliferation of another new technology: printed books, which opened up enormous opportunity for one person to wound and insult another via the printed word on the page, if not the screen. So there are technological continuities between their age and ours, but far deeper than that, there are also simple human continuities. Human nature has not budged over the intervening centuries, so the kind of dynamics we see at work in the breakdown of relationships back then are mirrored in our own present-day experience. What this means, of course, is that there are lessons for us to learn in those older divisions and disagreements. This book offers a detailed account of one relationship breakdown in particular and provides ample material to help us soberly reflect on our own differences or on those differences we see played out around us.

Those of us who count ourselves among the Christian community face the unsettling reality that the kinds of disagreements we witness in society at large also occur among our Christian brothers and sisters: even the most conscientious of Christians disagree. These are men and women who are respected and trusted. God seems to have blessed their life with fruitfulness. They may well be effective leaders or communicators. At a minimum, they are brothers and sisters who have been adopted into the family of God. They may also be part of the same group or congregation within the Christian church. They read the same Bible, with all its many encouragements and injunctions for unity. And yet they disagree. They do not get along. They fall out with each other.

Chances are, we have all seen instances of this disunity or been part of a controversy that has broken out even among fellow believers. Personalities clash. Disputes over beliefs arise. Changes in church practice create winners and losers. Wounds mount up; resentments accumulate. A follower of Jesus worships him in a Sunday morning service, all the while studiously avoiding a fellow believer just a few seats away. Or tensions reach the boiling point, spilling over into outright conflict with outbursts of hurt and anger. People leave; the church divides; relationships are never repaired. It seems it has been this way from the beginning. The apostle Paul had to rebuke the Christians in Corinth for dividing into rival factions (1 Cor. 3:1–4). The subsequent history of the church right down to the present day is littered with examples of disunity, division, fragmentation, and the very things that Paul warned against: "quarreling, jealousy, anger, hostility, slander, gossip, conceit, and disorder" (2 Cor. 12:20).

This is a difficult challenge to meet. Part of the problem is that we are too close, too invested in the disagreements we see around us. What we need is some distance and the objectivity to see things as they are and to discern all the different layers of what is really going on. One way of gaining that distance is by examining in detail a complex controversy we have no stake in, one that took place, in this case, nearly four hundred years ago. Richard Baxter (1615–1691) and John Owen (1616–1683) were two very important and respected leaders within seventeenth-century English Christianity. No one should doubt their godliness, their devotion to God, or their commitment to the cause of peace and unity. But they did not like each other, and we are about to see why. We will understand the multilayered reasons for their hostility and observe how their relationship—never bright to begin with—deteriorated over the decades, finally settling into a fixed and mutual dislike. Spoiler alert: there is no happy ending. This is a classic, timeless story no doubt repeated with minor variations countless times over the centuries but in this case one for which we have ample evidence. It offers an archetype of conflict between Christians that, for all the distance between them and us, is enduringly relevant to our own day.

The fact that their story is an old one is to our advantage. We have nothing at stake in these two men, so we can observe them dispassionately and objectively. We can identify patterns and draw lessons in the hope that we can apply them to our circumstances. The four hundred years of distance help separate us from the emotion of our own entanglements. Returning to our context, we might be able to see ourselves in a more detached fashion. Ordinarily, we are too close to our own conflict to easily understand the complex, unspoken, dimly recognized layers of what is actually taking place. Whether we are one of the protagonists or a disagreement is simply taking place around us, conflict is messy. It is difficult to see things clearly. But when we step back into the seventeenth century, we silence the emotional noise. In that relative stillness, it becomes possible to make observations and draw conclusions that serve us well as we return to the twenty-first century to negotiate our own context of conflict. That is my hope with this book.

I am very aware that for most of us, seventeenth-century England is a foreign country, so I have done my best to keep the story simple and accessible. Written for a popular Christian audience, this is a much shorter version of my earlier book for a scholarly audience, *John Owen, Richard Baxter, and the Formation of Non-conformity* (Ashgate, 2011). I am grateful to my good friend Michael Haykin for suggesting that I write a more accessible account. In this version, I have not said everything I might have said about this relationship. Anyone seeking the fuller story or more detailed evidence can consult that earlier book (I give some further guidance in the "Further Reading" section at the end of this book). When I quote from seventeenth-century sources, I have silently updated the language and grammar to a more contemporary English. In the first chapter, I have provided a brief outline of each man's life, one that emphasizes their similarities and positive qualities in a way that the subsequent chapters do not. There, the story unfolds in a little more detail. This makes some repetition inevitable in those following chapters, but I imagine the reader who is unfamiliar with the seventeenth century might appreciate the reinforcement. In the same vein, a glossary of key terms is available in the back matter if you would like to know more about what a word means. Also in the back matter is a chronology that provides a time line of events.

In putting the book together, I have been very conscious of my limitations as a historian—I am not a psychologist or a counselor, though I have been a church pastor. While I go on to offer my own reflections, I am determined to open up space for you to reflect on the story for yourself and to bring your own wisdom to bear. For that reason, I have ended each chapter (except the first) with a series of questions that you might ponder, either by yourself or in a small group. I have not given any indication of what I think the most important present-day issues of contention might be. For one thing, I do not want the book to become dated as issues that seem urgent and pressing today begin to fade and pass, to be replaced by other issues that come to dominate our minds tomorrow. For another, I want to empower you, the reader, to apply the lessons of this story to the issues that seem most important and obvious to you. The reality is that I have no easy answers. The tale I unfold presents us with any number of important questions, and I have left open as much space as possible for you to reflect and come to your own conclusions.

Perhaps I should offer a word of warning. We are about to learn why two men came to dislike each other so intensely. Here we see Owen and Baxter in their worst light, not in their best light—indeed, they brought out the worst in each other. This is not a flattering account. John Lardas Modern has said that "the burden of church history is, among other things, the call to converse more humanely with the dead."[1] I have no wish to denigrate these two men, but I do seek to interpret them accurately and humanely. This means taking account of the ways in which they were all too human and, I hope, not writing with any hint of condescension, as if I am somehow above the fallenness they shared. The point of their story is not so much that Christians disagree but how they go about their disagreement. It is really quite remarkable that mature believers who are, in so many respects, magnificent examples of what it means to follow Jesus with faithfulness and sincerity can also be Christians with pronounced blind spots who demonstrate brittleness, selfishness, and ego in their relationships with others and who damage those around them. We are all human; we are each a mixed bag. As Martin Luther once observed, we are sinners

---

1   John Lardas Modern, "The Burdens of Church History," *Church History* 83, no. 4 (2014): 990.

and saints all at the same time. Baxter and Owen are not going to come out of this book looking like saints. That is just not the story I need to tell. But let me place on record the high regard I have for both men. The achievements and the example they have left behind are mightily impressive. I would not have spent my life studying them if they were not worth studying. There is much to admire, and I do admire it, but my admiration must be the focus of a different book.

I am compelled to acknowledge a group of friends and readers who generously gave their time and insight to make this book far better than I could have made it on my own: Raewyn Booth, Kelvin Gardiner, Gareth Jones, and Joseph Wingfield. I am deeply, sincerely grateful for their responses and suggestions. If you find the end result at all readable, accessible, and helpful, much of the credit goes to them.

Here, then, are these two giant leaders of the seventeenth century, warts and all. They are a lived example of how even the most godly Christians disagree and do a pretty poor job of it and how relationships break down even between the most sincere believers. I hope their conflict can help us understand and manage our own difficulties with each other so that we might, as far as we possibly can while we live in this world, all be "of the same mind, having the same love, being in full accord and of one mind" (Phil. 2:2).

.

1

Two Good Men

WHEN THE RICH YOUNG RULER came to Jesus with his pressing question, addressing him as "Good Teacher," Jesus responded with a question of his own: "Why do you call me good? No one is good except God alone" (Luke 18:18–19). This is important. Only God is good; none of us are good. We have many fine qualities, to be sure, and we retain the image of God, but we are flawed, deeply flawed. Even the best of us is shot through with human sinfulness and frailty. We are all vulnerable to blind spots and besetting sins. Our best efforts are colored by imperfection. There are no exceptions. Only God is good.

Yet the evident truth of Jesus's observation does not prevent us from saying that someone is good: "He is a good man." "She is a good woman." We know what we mean. We do not intend to convey that such a man or woman is a model of perfection, but there is something about each one that we can say is genuinely good. Within the confines of human weakness, they are doing their best. They stand out for their presence and contribution.

In these terms, John Owen and Richard Baxter were two good men. There is much to admire in their character and achievements. Even today, four centuries on, a great many contemporary Christians hold them in high esteem. In this first chapter, I want to sketch out their life story to introduce these men to you in such a way as to emphasize their many positive qualities, accomplishments, and commonalities. That is because the remaining chapters, necessarily, accentuate the negatives and draw attention to their differences. Neither man comes out of this book looking that great. While we can say that they were both good men, we must add that "no one is good except God alone."

Early Formation

Baxter and Owen had a lot in common. To begin with, they were both Puritans, which means they were deeply committed to seeing the Church of England reformed according to the prescription laid out in the pages of the New Testament. The label of "Puritan" was deployed against them as an insult. Baxter referred to it as "the odious name," and no one liked being called a Puritan.[1] They preferred to label themselves "the godly" or "the saints." The nickname comes from the word "purity": Puritans sought to purify the Church of England from anything that was a merely human innovation and to see the church return to its pure form in the age of the apostles. Over the centuries, "corruption" had crept into the church as its worship and leadership structures had become ever more elaborate and complex. For the Puritans, that corruption was embodied most comprehensively in the Roman Catholic Church.

1   Richard Baxter, *Reliquiae Baxterianae, or, Mr. Richard Baxter's Narrative of the Most Memorable Passages of His Life and Times*, ed. Matthew Sylvester (London, 1696), 1:2.

Inheritors of the sixteenth-century Reformation, the Puritans sought to re-create the initial simplicity of the church in its earliest and purest form. They also tried to purify the society around them, publicly attacking such sins as swearing, drunkenness, sexual immorality, and the failure to acknowledge Sunday as the Sabbath, a day of rest from work but filled for them with activity such as church services, prayer meetings, and discussions of the day's sermons. Indeed, Puritans loved their sermons. They revered the Scriptures and traveled many miles to hear them preached—and not just on Sunday. But their tendency to attack sin on a societal and national level did not endear them to their "ungodly" neighbors.

Owen and Baxter were both born into the Puritan tradition, and they were born at pretty much the same time: Baxter on Sunday, November 12, 1615; Owen sometime in 1616. Baxter was raised in the county of Shropshire, far to the west of London in the Midlands near the border with Wales. For reasons he did not explain, he lived with his maternal grandfather for the first ten years of his life before moving to live with his parents. He was an only child in a family that privileged Puritan piety. Baxter shared in that piety from an early age, persuaded that the seriousness with which his parents pursued their faith by far excelled the much more profane way of life he witnessed in the community around him. Owen, one of at least six children, was also raised in a devoutly Puritan household, in the village of Stadham (today, Stadhampton), about six miles from Oxford. His father was a deeply conscientious minister in the Church of England.

Owen received an excellent education. While young, he attended a school that met in a private home within All Saints Parish in Oxford. In 1628 he entered Queen's College, Oxford, at the age of twelve, which was not an unusually young age to begin university study in those days. Four years later he graduated with a bachelor of arts. In 1635 he graduated with a master of arts. England's two universities (the other being Cambridge University) trained England's ministers. By the time Owen graduated with his MA, both universities were well into a period of reform led by the archbishop of Canterbury, who was also chancellor of Oxford University, William Laud. These reforms tended to pull both the Church of England and Oxford University away from its Calvinist moorings toward a style of theology and ceremony that seemed worryingly Roman Catholic to England's staunch Protestants. Unhappy with these developments, Owen left Oxford in 1637. This was no easy decision. It seems that this transition threw him into a state of depression (he withdrew from human interaction entirely "and very hardly could be induced to speak a word").[2] While its intensity lasted only around three months, the aftereffects lingered for several years.

Baxter's education took an entirely different path. He attended a few mediocre schools in his locality, but he did not go on to university. He was persuaded to take up the offer of learning under a private tutor, who, in the event, proved wholly inadequate. But he did provide the young Baxter with two things conducive to his education: plenty of books and plenty of time to read them. Thus Baxter was an autodidact (that is, he was self-taught), but we should not underestimate his intelligence or his education. If anything, his self-discipline and lifelong inclination

2 John Asty, "Memoirs of the Life of John Owen," in *A Complete Collection of the Sermons of the Reverend and Learned John Owen.* [. . .] *And to the Whole Are Prefixed Memoirs of His Life*, ed. John Asty (London: John Clark, 1721), 4.

to compensate for his lack of university training made him only more studious and industrious. He certainly never lost his early love of reading books (and writing them!). Both he and Owen possessed a formidable intelligence, and both would deploy their considerable intellectual and literary abilities in the service of God.

Indeed, both men developed a genuine, personal faith, if again in different ways. For Baxter, he discerned a deepening awareness of God's call on his life, even though still very young, but there was no single, decisive moment he could point to. "Whether sincere conversion began now, or before, or after" that season of general discernment, he said, "I was never able to this day to know."[3] Not so with Owen. While there is no doubting his grounding in the faith from an early age, what we might call a moment of conversion came sometime around 1642 as he listened to a sermon preached at Aldermanbury Church in London by an otherwise unremarkable and anonymous preacher. The text was Matthew 8:26, "Why are you afraid, O you of little faith?" and the sermon spoke directly to Owen's condition. In the words of his early biographer, "God designed to speak peace to his soul."[4] The effects of his depression lifted, and he became firmly assured of grace and grounded in his faith.

Pastoral Ministry, Civil War, and Early Publications

Owen and Baxter entered the 1640s as sincere, thoughtful, and well-educated young men of around twenty-five years old, but they ventured into full adulthood at a time of growing national tension. After a century of rising inflation, the amount of taxation

3 Baxter, *Reliquiae Baxterianae*, 1:3.
4 Asty, "Memoirs of the Life of John Owen," 5.

approved by Parliament was inadequate to fund the costs of the crown. In response, King Charles I simply bypassed Parliament to pursue other means of raising revenue that were considered by many to be illegal and unconstitutional. Among the most contentious was "ship money," a tax usually imposed on coastal towns in a time of war. In October 1634 Charles imposed ship money in a time of peace; a year later he extended the tax to inland towns. He did not summon Parliament at all from March 1629 to April 1640 in what are now called the eleven years of "personal rule," thus clamping shut one of the most important pressure valves in representing legitimate grievance against the government. During that period, Charles and his archbishop of Canterbury, William Laud, also clamped down on Puritan Nonconformity in the parishes. Ministers who refused to use the Book of Common Prayer or wear the surplice (a loose vestment of white linen that many Puritans viewed as a Roman Catholic hangover) were fined, removed from office, or imprisoned. This was the decade when many Puritans fled to New England, where they could shape a church to their liking without the interference of bishops. Those who remained felt increasingly persecuted and alienated.

Worse still, in 1637 Charles and Laud attempted to impose the same kind of conformity in Scotland. Charles was king of England, Scotland, and Ireland, and ruling multiple kingdoms posed a challenge for even the very best of politicians. Charles was not the best of politicians. His attempt to impose Church of England conformity on the Church of Scotland was a disaster. In 1639 many of his Scottish subjects rebelled, and the Scottish army invaded the north of England. Now in desperate need of money to meet the incursion, Charles had no choice but to call

Parliament in April 1640. Only one month later, he dissolved what is known as the "Short Parliament," but he was forced to summon the "Long Parliament" in November 1640 after the Scots successfully invaded a second time, demanding £850 a day until the conclusion of a formal peace treaty.

With Parliament back in being, the long-pent-up flood of grievance now erupted. Charles had lost the trust of many of his people. He had imposed illegal taxation, infringed on the people's liberties, and enacted a religious policy that looked alarmingly Catholic. With a Catholic wife, Henrietta Maria of France, who kept a Catholic chapel at court in London, it was not inconceivable that England's king might reestablish Catholicism, by force if necessary. Then in October 1641, the Irish Catholics rose up in rebellion against their Protestant landlords. The rumor that Charles himself had sponsored the uprising gained broad credence. Deeply distrustful of the king, Parliament took control of the various militias organized to suppress the Irish. Charles gathered his own forces, and in October 1642, actual fighting broke out, the beginning of four years of the brutal, pervasive, and devastating English Civil War. What Parliament hoped at the beginning would be only a short campaign sufficient for compelling the king to negotiate a permanent settlement turned into four years of extended bitterness, division, and misery. Around 868,000 people died (from conflicts including not only the war in 1642–1646 but also the fighting outside England [in Scotland and Ireland] and the later periods of conflict in 1648 and 1649–1651) either in the actual violence of battle or in the disease and deprivation that followed armed soldiers around the countryside. That is a proportion of around 11 percent in a population of somewhere near 7.5 million (in contrast, around 2.5 percent of the population died during the American Civil War).[5] The fighting took place from one end of England to the other, leaving almost no part of the country unscathed. The upheaval and devastation can only be imagined. Only when Parliament's various military forces were reforged into one "New Model Army" at the beginning of 1645 did the tide of the war turn against Charles. He finally surrendered on May 5, 1646.

These events affected the course of life for both Owen and Baxter. Owen had been ordained a deacon in December 1632 and a priest in December 1638 before serving as a private chaplain in two successive family homes, then moving to London in 1642 and facing an unknown future. There, on the back of his newfound assurance of faith, he launched his writing career, publishing *A Display of Arminianism* in 1643. Arminianism (named after the Dutch theologian Jacobus Arminius) is the name given to the style of doctrine then preferred by both King Charles and William Laud, one that emphasized human choice and moral responsibility in salvation over against the accent on God's choice, predestination, and election that underpinned the previously prevailing Calvinism (named after the Genevan pastor and theologian John Calvin). Owen's book relentlessly dismantled the supporting structures of Arminianism and defended Reformed orthodoxy

5 For casualties from the British Civil Wars, see Charles Carlton, *Going to the Wars: The Experience of the British Civil Wars, 1638–1651* (London: Routledge, 1992), 214. For casualties from the American Civil War, J. David Hacker notes, "The most probable number of deaths attributable to the [American] Civil War is 752,000," while the United States Census Bureau reports a population of 31,443,321 in the 1860 census. Hacker, "A Census-Based Count of the Civil War Dead," *Civil War History* 57, no. 4 (2011): 307; United States Census Bureau, "Decennial Census Official Publications: 1860," last modified December 16, 2021, https://www.census.gov/.

(that is, the theology of the Swiss Reformation that did much to shape the sixteenth-century Church of England after its break with Rome). Owen dedicated it to the members of the Committee for Religion in the House of Lords. They rewarded him with his first ministerial position in the parish of Fordham in the county of Essex, nearly seventy miles to the northeast of London.

Thus began seven years of pastoral ministry first at Fordham and then, from 1646, at the parish of Coggeshall. This second post involved a move of only eight miles, but Coggeshall was a much larger parish, around two thousand people on a Sunday morning, with a proud Puritan heritage. In those years he published two further works. *The Duty of Pastors and People Distinguished* (1644) presented his thoughts on the way the church ought to be structured. *The Principles of the Doctrine of Christ* (1645) comprised two catechisms, each a series of questions and answers designed to be memorized for the understanding of basic Christian doctrine by children and adults (as a requirement for receiving Communion). This volume indicates Owen's commitment to effective and painstaking pastoral investment. In his dedication to the book, he reminded his parishioners how he had taught them publicly and "from house to house," an allusion to Paul's speech to the Ephesian elders in Acts 20:18–35.[6] Owen's promotion to Coggeshall shows that he must have been considered a very effective pastor and preacher.

Baxter's experience of the 1640s also began with pastoral ministry. He had been ordained a deacon in 1638, completed a brief stint as a school teacher, served for a short while at Bridgnorth

---

6   John Owen, *The Principles of the Doctrine of Christ* (London, 1645), sig. A2v.

as an assistant to the vicar, and then in April 1641 accepted an invitation to become the preacher or "lecturer" in the parish of Kidderminster in the neighboring county of Worcestershire. There he would make his name but not before the civil war intervened and national divisions took a very personal turn. Late in the summer of 1642, he left Kidderminster for a month in the face of local opposition. His return was short lived. The threat of violence forced him out again at the end of October, driven "by the insurrection of a rabble that with clubs sought to kill me."[7]

The Midlands was Royalist territory and unsympathetic to the cause of Parliament, let alone the cause of the Puritans, and Baxter supported both. Now unsettled and homeless, Baxter sought refuge with the parliamentary garrison at the city of Coventry. He remained there for over two years, preaching to the soldiers in return for room and board. He was at that time relatively sheltered, but he could not avoid the almost daily news of disaster or death from somewhere or other as the war dragged on. In June 1645 he visited some friends in Parliament's army the day after their victory at the battle of Naseby. He was horrified by the dangerous doctrine he found circulating among his friends—dangerous because it seemed to imply that Christian believers could live as they liked and sin as much as they pleased without placing their salvation in peril. He resolved to join the army as a chaplain in the regiment of Colonel Edward Whalley. Baxter joined Whalley's soldiers as they traveled England mopping up the last sites of resistance as the war at last turned decisively in Parliament's favor. Even after Charles surrendered in May 1646, Baxter remained as

---

7 Baxter to Stephen Lobb, June 9 and 16, 1684, Baxter Correspondence, Dr. Williams's Library, vol. 2, fol. 93.

an army chaplain until February 1647, when his health collapsed and he very nearly died.

That crisis of ill health triggered his writing career. Expecting imminent death, he began to write what he called his "funeral sermon," presumably a gathering of his final thoughts to preach to himself. But he did not die. Instead, he kept writing, and what he initially intended as a brief sermon grew into his massive and enduring devotional work *The Saints' Everlasting Rest*. In that work, which wasn't published until 1650, Baxter encouraged his readers to emulate his practice of meditating daily on their future rest in heaven. In counterpoint to that perpetual joy, the grim horror of his civil war experience regularly intrudes on his reflection. Baxter emerged from those war years with a lingering sense of trauma, and his bestselling book was a tonic for his fellow citizens trying to make sense of a confusing and frightening world.

A second book emerged from his near-death experience, *Aphorisms of Justification*, which appeared in 1649, his first published work. As he was writing his funeral sermon, he reflected on Matthew 25, where Christ appears to judge the sheep and the goats on the basis of their works. In a moment of blinding illumination, inspiration, and clarity, a new understanding of salvation slipped into place. Baxter devised a new system that retained the Calvinist understanding of predestination and the infallible salvation of the elect alongside a central place for human responsibility. The first 10 pages of *Aphorisms of Justification* offer a ringing endorsement of Calvinist doctrine. The remaining 325 pages erect an extensive series of hedges to prevent readers from ever assuming that such doctrine means they can live as they please: repentance, obedience, and lifelong perseverance all play a part, if an infinitesimally small one, in the salvation of every believer. Baxter's project was not well received. While *The Saints' Everlasting Rest* quickly became a devotional classic, still in print today, *Aphorisms of Justification* aroused notoriety and controversy. But that dispute was still in the future in May 1647, when Baxter returned to Kidderminster to pick up the threads of his earlier ministry, with impressive results.

The Heights of Influence

Both Owen and Baxter came into their own during the 1650s. Owen had forged important connections on a national scale, even preaching before Parliament just as Charles surrendered in late April 1646, and he preached again on January 31, 1649, the day after the execution of the king. That decisive act began the Interregnum, the time between the reigns of Charles I and Charles II, eleven years in which England remained a republic (that is, the monarchy was abolished). Owen's third sermon to Parliament in April 1649 brought him into direct contact with the foremost political figure of the Interregnum, Oliver Cromwell. Owen became one of Cromwell's chaplains and followed him first to Ireland (where Owen focused mainly on reordering Trinity College, Dublin) and then to Scotland. He also became a chaplain to the Council of State, the executive body that governed England alongside Parliament.

During the 1650s Owen was a figure of national influence in three main ways. First, he became dean of Christ Church at Oxford University in 1651 and vice-chancellor of the university in 1653, energetically pursuing a series of reforms designed ultimately to improve the quality and Reformed theology of England's ministers in training.

Second, he was one of the leading architects of a new religious settlement. He helped establish a system for approving all ministers who met raised expectations for ministry and theology and for removing those ministers who failed to meet the required standard. He also worked hard—but ultimately unsuccessfully—to gain Parliament's approval for a new doctrinal basis for the Church of England, one that identified the essential beliefs of the Christian faith and therefore set the bounds of those Christian groups who would be tolerated in an environment of expanded religious freedom. In particular, Owen was a leading figure (likely *the* leading figure) in a small group of ministers summoned to advise Parliament on a new religious settlement in late 1654. As we will see, Baxter was part of the same group.

The final main way that Owen exerted his influence was as an author. By the end of 1659, he had published thirty-four books that ranged across a number of important devotional subjects as well as issues of contemporary controversy. We might note in particular his massive *Vindiciae Evangelicae, or, The Mystery of the Gospel Vindicated*. Commissioned by Parliament and published in 1655, this work attacked an emerging and alarming theological variant by the name of Socinianism. Taken from the name of an Italian theologian, Faustus Socinus, Socinianism denied many of the foundational beliefs of orthodox Christianity, such as the Trinity and the deity of Christ, and placed Christian understandings of the gospel itself in peril. Thus Owen served as England's theological heavy hitter—a nationally acknowledged defender of Christian orthodoxy brought in to demolish a worrying new heresy.

Baxter also rose to national prominence during the 1650s. By 1659 *The Saints' Everlasting Rest* (first published in 1650) had appeared in its eighth edition; it was what we would call a runaway bestseller, and by the end of the decade, he had published a total of thirty-seven books. While his controversial writings had attracted an astonishing array of critics, his more devotional and practical works were widely appreciated. As an illustration of his reach as a highly regarded author, the first book after the Bible that the missionary to the Native Americans John Eliot translated into the Massachusetts language was Baxter's *Call to the Unconverted*, in 1664. Across his many publications, he dealt pastorally and effectively with almost every conceivable aspect of the Christian life, charging his readers to orient their lives to the call of God and an eternal future of heavenly rest that made all the attractions of this world fade into insignificance.

Baxter built his reputation on the back of genuine credibility in pastoral ministry in his parish of Kidderminster: he turned the town around. As he later explained, when he arrived he was lucky to find even one godly family living on each street, but by the close of the 1650s, the proportions had been reversed. This success rested on a combination of excellent preaching and painstaking pastoral care. The parish had to build five extra galleries of seating just to accommodate the expanded congregation within the church building. Like all Puritans, Baxter placed a premium on preaching, and he put enormous effort into what he preached and how he preached. But he also believed that preaching in itself was not enough to bring believers to full maturity. He developed an intentional model of individual soul care in which he and his assistant would devote two whole days each week (including the evenings) to meet for one hour with every willing family in the parish once a year. In those conversations, he used a catechism to assess the faith and understanding of each person. These sessions were in their own way minisermons, couched in the back-and-forth of everyday conversation and crafted to the particular needs of each individual. Thus, like Owen, Baxter employed a catechism for the purpose of meeting Paul's injunction to the Ephesian elders in Acts 20:28 to "pay careful attention . . . to all the flock." He worked tirelessly for the good of those under his care. Under his leadership, Kidderminster was steadily reformed.

His vision extended beyond just his own parish. England had a divided church. Even among Puritans, fault lines had visibly widened under the pressure of the civil war and its aftermath. After his own traumatic experience of the war, Baxter longed for order and peace, and he developed a lifelong yearning to bring Christians together in unity. He identified four main parties within the English church (Congregationalists, Episcopalians, Erastians, and Presbyterians), but he felt that the moderates within each party held similar views and, more importantly, could work together in practice even if their principles varied. He believed that if England's ministers simply got on with the work of ministry, they would be too busy to notice how their differing doctrines of church government might otherwise keep them apart. So he formed the Worcestershire Association, a network open to local parish ministers of all stripes who met monthly for the purpose of mutual edification and encouragement. In 1653 they published their agreement to work together, and similar ministerial associations sprang up in other counties. In 1656 Baxter published *The Reformed Pastor*, the second of his classic works still in print today. That book pitched his vision for pastoral ministry to the whole nation. By the end of the decade, Baxter had reason to hope that the kind of reformation he had witnessed in Kidderminster would be replicated in thousands of other parishes across the whole country. But it was not to be. Just as he felt his dreams might be moving toward reality, they collapsed in dust and ruin.

Disappointment and Dark Times

Baxter began the year 1659 full of optimism. Oliver Cromwell, England's Lord Protector, had died a few months earlier. His son Richard was much more to Baxter's liking. He dedicated not just one but two books to the new Protector, welcoming him as a new King Solomon, whom God had kept apart from bloodshed in order to bring about national peace and prosperity (see 1 Chron. 22:6–10). Under Richard Cromwell's leadership, England was ripe for reformation along the lines of what Baxter had witnessed in Kidderminster. But the army leaders had other ideas. In April they engineered what was in effect a coup d'état, and the following month Richard resigned as Lord Protector. These events preempted months of political instability and increasing chaos that were resolved finally by the restoration of the monarchy and the return of King Charles II in May 1660. Owen would have been just as disappointed as Baxter by this reversal of fortune, though Owen occupied a different place in those events. In 1659 he was a chaplain to those leaders of the army that had brought down Richard Cromwell. For someone like Owen, who had attached so much significance and promise to what he saw as God's many great works of providence in Parliament's victory in the civil war, the Restoration presented a bewildering, confusing, and utterly dispiriting reality. Had God really worked such wonders—and now all for nothing?

Worse still, both men were on the back foot politically just as the restored bishops of the Church of England quickly surged to political dominance. Given that he had preached to Parliament the day after the execution of King Charles I, Owen owed a debt to his political connections for avoiding execution himself as others involved in the regicide met a grisly end. For Baxter and those moderate Puritans like him who hoped for a broad, inclusive, and reformed Church of England, the restored bishops gave nothing away. Parliament passed the Act of Uniformity in 1662, which required all ministers in the Church of England to agree to everything in the Book of Common Prayer, the volume that provided the liturgy used in the Church of England. No sincere Puritan could easily do that in good conscience, and around two thousand ministers lost their ministerial position. The effect was to thrust them and their families into poverty. Thus began what Baxter called "the great inundation of calamities": nearly thirty years of persecuting, at varying levels, those who sought to enact a Puritan vision for the Church of England, a vision now thoroughly repudiated by those in charge of the church.[8] Baxter would find himself in prison twice, and thousands of others were fined or imprisoned for breaches of legislation with increasingly severe penalties.

With the Restoration came a change of leadership among Puritans as one generation laid aside the burden for others like Baxter and Owen, now in their mid-forties, to pick up. These two men became, in effect, the leaders of their respective stream among the Puritans (now called Dissenters or Nonconformists).

8   Baxter, *Reliquiae Baxterianae*, 2:385.

Baxter was the leading figure among the Presbyterians, those who continued to hope for a broad and inclusive Church of England that would encompass moderate Puritan sensibilities. Owen was the leading figure among the Congregationalists, those who were comfortable enough sitting outside the structure of the Church of England and who sought only toleration of their existence and freedom from legal sanction. It is not as if these two men held any sort of formal office, nor that they were alone in leading these respective streams, but it fell largely to them to shepherd those of a similar mind through difficult times and to represent their interests in crucial conversations at a national level. Baxter occupied no formal place of ministry and was careful not to fall foul of legislative requirements. He turned to writing to carry on his pastoral ministry, publishing in total around 140 books over the course of his life. Owen also continued to write, publishing over 70 books by the time of his death, and he managed to carry on an active pastoral ministry to a small congregation in London. He battled on doggedly, in print and preaching, defending the gospel and genuinely fearing not just its loss but the reimposition of Roman Catholicism in England. Both men were nothing if not faithful to the very end.

And so they died, Owen in 1683, Baxter in 1691. What we say at funerals is always in danger of overstating the positive qualities of the deceased, but even so, we catch a glimpse of these two men in the sermons preached at their funerals. David Clarkson mourned the absence of Owen's leadership: "We have lost an excellent pilot when we have most need of him, when a fierce storm is coming upon us, and I dread the consequences of it." He pleaded with God to make up their loss in light of Owen's massive contribution: "He had extraordinary intellectuals, a clear and piercing judgment. He was a passionate lover of light and truth, and he pursued divine truth so unweariedly, through careful writing and study, that it impaired his health and strength." He lamented that "a great light has fallen, one of eminency for holiness and learning, and pastoral abilities; a pastor, a scholar, a skilful minister of the first magnitude."[9]

In a similar fashion, William Bates spoke warmly of Baxter's example, contribution, and leadership, and he reflected on his humility in the last years of his life:

> Never was a sinner more humble and debasing himself, never was a sincere believer more calm and comfortable. He acknowledged himself to be the vilest dunghill-worm (that was his usual expression) that ever went to heaven. He admired God's condescension to us, often saying, "Lord, what is man, what am I, vile worm, to the great God?" Many times he prayed, "God be merciful to me a sinner." He said, "God may justly condemn me for the best duty I ever did, and all my hopes are from the free mercy of God in Christ," which he often prayed for.[10]

Bates recalled that when someone praised Baxter for his many publications, he replied with the same humility: "I was but a pen in God's hand, and what praise is due to a pen?"[11]

---

9 David Clarkson, "A Funeral Sermon on the Much Lamented Death of John Owen," in *Seventeen Sermons Preached by the Late Reverend and Learned John Owen* (London, 1720), 1:71, 72, 74–75.

10 William Bates, *A Funeral Sermon for Richard Baxter*, 2nd ed. (London, 1692), 124–25.

11 Bates, *Funeral Sermon*, 125.

These were, then, in the accounts of those who knew them best, two good men. Steadfast and prodigious across the whole span of life, each one sought to serve God and his people faithfully and fittingly. And this was no easy life: the trauma of civil war, fleeting success, and decades of demanding leadership in dark times. These were good men who have earned our respect. But they were not perfect men. As you are about to find out, they had their dark side, their blind spots, their sins, flaws, and fallibilities, as we all do. More than that, for all that they had in common and for all that might have thrown them together, they did not like each other, and they did not get along. They were Christian brothers who profoundly disagreed with each other, and their disagreement contributed to the ongoing division among sincere Christians of the seventeenth century. We now turn to the story of their disagreement in the hope that with the distance we have from the seventeenth century, we can learn some lessons that might help us navigate and mitigate the divisions of our own day. May God bring light to our minds and humility to our hearts.

2

Experience

WE TEND TO THINK of ourselves as autonomous individuals firmly in control of our own decision-making, finding our way in the world through the choices we make, both large and small. While this is true to a significant extent, it is not an entirely safe assumption. It overlooks the ways in which we have been profoundly shaped by forces that lie outside our control. We do not choose the family into which we are born, our DNA, our prenatal environment, the quality of nurture we receive in our early years, or the shaping forces in our social, political, and cultural context as we grow into maturity. All that life experience molds how we see the world and how we perceive both ourselves and others. When two people come into conflict, they bring with them a contrasting set of perspectives informed by their respective pasts. Their personal history is very much alive. It operates in ways that they themselves may not recognize, let alone the person with whom they have clashed. Thus, two people can be set up for conflict and misunderstanding before they even meet.

So it was with Richard Baxter and John Owen. They did not choose to live in seventeenth-century England; they were simply born there and born then. Nor did they choose to live through a civil war; it came to them. Yet even though they both supported Parliament, they experienced the war in starkly contrasting ways. In this chapter, we consider their differing experience of the war and begin to think more carefully about how previous life experience can shape our ongoing relationships, for better or worse.

Baxter's Civil War

For Baxter, England's civil war started early and lasted long. Kidderminster lay in the Midlands, which was firmly Royalist territory, and the tensions were evident even before any fighting began. In one instance, Baxter was publicly labeled a traitor; on other occasions, he was denounced as a "Roundhead" (a popular nickname for those who supported Parliament's cause, possibly based on their short, sober hairstyle). His friends advised him to leave town for his own safety. After a month in Gloucester, he returned to Kidderminster only to be forced out again, fearing for his life. Thus began nearly five years of dislocation. It is important to appreciate how unnerving and unsettling that experience would be.

For one thing, Baxter witnessed the violence of war at close range. The very first physical skirmish took place at Powick Bridge, just south of Worcester, on September 23, 1642. It was an ambush, unplanned and spontaneous, and yet remarkably, Baxter was on hand to witness it. Having never seen an army before, his curiosity prompted him to leave the safety of nearby Inkborough (today, Inkberrow) to view a small force of Parliament's soldiers. He watched as they crossed the bridge. He observed them flee from the Royalist soldiers who pounced on them on the other side. "This sight quickly told me the vanity of Armies, and how little confidence is to be placed in them."[1] More sobering still, Baxter was preaching at Alcester precisely one month later. He and his congregation could hear in the distance the cannon fire of the first major battle of the war at Edgehill. When he visited the site the next day, he saw a thousand dead bodies strewn across the battlefield. We might well ponder the grisly reality of that unprecedented scene. That horrifying, disturbing vision stayed with him for the rest of his days.

With the fighting now fully underway, Baxter spent the next two years in Coventry preaching to the parliamentary garrison in return for food and board. This period of relative stability and safety ended in June 1645, when he visited some friends among Parliament's soldiers at nearby Naseby. The army had just won a decisive battle that helped turn the course of the war. Even so, Baxter was dismayed. It seems that his friends had drifted into bad doctrine that had infected not just them but the whole army. They now believed that the provision of God's free grace in Christ and the full forgiveness of sins even from before they were born meant that they could live as they pleased. Horrified, Baxter joined the army as a chaplain to combat this disturbing new doctrine among the soldiers. The work involved him in another order of warfare entirely, yet it still brought him face-to-face with physical violence. As he followed the army around the countryside, he witnessed several of the remaining battles and sieges of the war. Battles were bad enough; sieges were appalling, brutal, and prolonged. They all left their mark on him. In February 1647 his health collapsed.

---

1   Richard Baxter, *Reliquiae Baxterianae, or, Mr. Richard Baxter's Narrative of the Most Memorable Passages of His Life and Times*, ed. Matthew Sylvester (London, 1696), 1:42.

When his nose started to bleed, he followed the conventional medical wisdom of the day and opened four veins in the hope of ridding his body of what appeared to be an excess of blood. The result nearly killed him. It ended his career as a chaplain, and he spent the next few months recuperating.

As we will see in chapter 4, this crisis proved decisive for the development of Baxter's own theology. For now, we might consider the mournful effects of this dismal war experience on his perspective. It colors the first book he began to write, *The Saints' Everlasting Rest*, which he eventually published in 1650. The main aim of the book was to encourage his readers to meditate daily on heaven. That is largely because his experience of earth had been so unremittingly awful of late. "Look on England's four years' blood," he wrote. Ruin lay all around. "Nothing appears to our sight but ruin: families ruined, congregations ruined, sumptuous structures ruined, cities ruined, country ruined, court ruined, and kingdoms ruined."[2] Clearly, all those stark images of devastating sieges, brutal warfare, and scattered corpses had stayed in his mind.

> Oh, the sad and heart-piercing spectacles that my eyes have seen in four years of civil war: in this fight a dear friend falls down by me; from another battle a precious Christian is brought home wounded or dead; scarcely a month, hardly a week without the sight or noise of blood, . . . the earth covered with the carcasses of the slain.[3]

2 Richard Baxter, *The Saints' Everlasting Rest*, 1st ed. (London, 1650), 122; cf. Richard Baxter, *The Saints' Everlasting Rest*, updated and abridged by Tim Cooper (Wheaton, IL: Crossway, 2022), 67.

3 Baxter, *Saints' Everlasting Rest* (1650), 123; cf. 2022 Crossway abridgment, 67–68.

These were just some of the "miseries of the late unhappy war."[4] He also discerned the disturbing effect of national events on the cause of the gospel. He lamented "the disappointed reformation, the hideous doctrines, and unheard-of wickedness" produced by war.[5] The proliferation of heresy and error personified in his friends at Naseby had subverted the gospel: "Oh, what abundance of excellent, hopeful fruits of godliness have I seen blown down before they were ripe, by the impetuous winds of war." The result: disaster for the Christian faith in England. "In a word," he concluded, "I never yet saw the work of the Gospel go on well in wars."[6]

Owen's Civil War

Where Baxter perceived the civil war as a disaster for the gospel in England, Owen saw it as a triumph. Their perspectives could hardly have been more different. We can trace that difference to one factor over which they had little control: geography. Geography matters. It certainly mattered in the war. The most intense fighting took place in the Midlands, where Baxter lived. But if we move to the southeast and draw a line running north to south from King's Lynn through Cambridge and London and on down to Arundel, we see a different story. Those living east of that line experienced relative calm. Of the 563 known incidents in the war, only one took place in Essex. That was where Owen spent most of the war.

---

4 Baxter, *Saints' Everlasting Rest* (1650), epistle dedicatory, sig. A2.
5 Richard Baxter, *The Saints' Everlasting Rest*, 2nd ed. (London, 1651), dedication of the whole, sig. a2.
6 Baxter, *Saints' Everlasting Rest* (1650), 524.

His experience of the war was, therefore, completely different from Baxter's. Owen passed through relatively unscathed and untroubled. Certainly, he experienced nothing like the itinerancy Baxter endured, nor, as far as we know, did he witness any actual violence. Baxter, living in Royalist territory, had been thrust out of his home when his pastoral ministry had barely begun. In contrast, Owen settled into productive ministry, first at Fordham, then at Coggeshall. So the war was abstract for him in a way that it could never be for Baxter, and he wholeheartedly supported its aims. Parliament worked to restore Calvinist doctrine to the heart of the Church of England. On January 10, 1645, it executed William Laud, the archbishop of Canterbury. A little over a year later, it had won the war.

Just at that point, in April 1646, Owen appeared on a national stage when he preached his first sermon to Parliament. Titled *A Vision of Unchangeable Free Mercy*, his sermon gloried in the recent war, which had liberated the gospel in England from its Arminian bondage. Now "the reformation of England [would] be more glorious than of any nation in the world," as long as the country held its new course away from Egypt and on to the promised land. So he warned against two sorts of men. The first would urge exactly that: a return to Egypt and a revival of Arminian theology. The second sort were those who could not see clearly, whose perspective was distorted: they "have gotten false glasses, representing all things unto them in dubious colors." Instead of glory and triumph, "they can see nothing but errors—errors of all sizes, sorts, sects and sexes—errors and heresies from the beginning to the end."[7] They

---

7 John Owen, *A Vision of Unchangeable Free Mercy* (1646), in *The Works of John Owen*, ed. William H. Goold, 16 vols. (1850–1853; repr., Edinburgh: Banner of Truth, 1983), 8:27–28.

were like men who look out on a field of corn and see only the weeds. This is a fascinating description. It is impossible to know exactly whom Owen had in mind, but this is a perfect description of Baxter, a man he had never even met.

Contrasting Perspectives

Both Baxter and Owen supported Parliament's cause in the civil war; they were on the same side. Yet their perspectives on the war provide a study in contrast.

For Owen, it represented the triumphant vindication of a glorious cause. The gospel had been rescued from its captivity, and a glorious national reformation seemed imminent. Beyond the turmoil of human affairs, God himself had moved in power. "Oh Lord, how was England of late, by your mercy, delivered from this snare," he exclaimed in his sermon to Parliament. "Oh how has your grace fought against our backsliding!"[8] The war had been England's redemption and worth any cost: "If there had been no difficulties, there had been no deliverances." To his mind, any reasonable person would surely see that this moment of sheer triumph "was cheaply purchased by yesterday's anguish and fear."[9] He compared that former anxiety to mere seasickness experienced on a voyage from a dark place to a brighter one. It is true that Owen's task was to preach a sermon to boost morale in a time of crisis, but even so, only someone who had avoided the horrors of the war could speak so calmly about them. It is unlikely that anyone who lost a loved one in the fighting would agree that the gains had been "cheaply purchased"; the trauma of the war was

8 Owen, *Free Mercy*, in Owen, *Works*, 8:25.
9 Owen, *Free Mercy*, in Owen, *Works*, 8:18.

no trifling, transitory seasickness. It is not that Owen was necessarily trite or complacent about the war, but it had not been his firsthand experience as it had for someone like Baxter. This gave Owen much greater freedom to focus on the strategic objectives of the war without their clarity being muddied by the harsh reality of the carnage it caused.

Baxter never enjoyed such a luxury. If England was a cornfield, he was down among the weeds and could see only the weeds. His metaphor was rather different from Owen's, though no less agricultural. England's inhabitants were like a pond that begrudges the banks that constrain it, "and therefore combine with the winds to raise a tempest, and so assault and break down the banks in their rage." Where, he now asked, "is that peaceable association of waters?"[10] This is a much more ominous image. A body of water is a massive, uncontrollable thing, and once the damage is done, it cannot be repaired. One is powerless in the face of it; mere weeds, however rampant, can at least be pared back.

Furthermore, we have seen that while Owen had little doubt, Baxter was much less certain about what the war achieved, if anything constructive at all. Owen saw the war as a welcome liberation of the gospel; Baxter saw only its corruption and demise. Owen felt England to be on the brink of a glorious reformation; Baxter felt that the Reformation had been jettisoned. Owen testified to the freedom of the gospel, newly rescued from the Arminian snare; Baxter perceived only "the Gospel departing." Both looked for the hand of God in contemporary events, yet they interpreted that hand in starkly different ways. Owen was convinced that

10 Baxter, *Saints' Everlasting Rest* (1650), 520–21.

"all things here below," especially where the gospel is concerned, take place "according to the regular motions and goings forth of God's free, eternal, unchangeable decree."[11] Owen easily rose above the chaos of war to see how God had been moving against the Arminians to defeat them, to frustrate their plans, and to rescue the gospel from its captivity. But that was much harder, if not impossible, for Baxter. When he looked for the hand of God, he offered a drastically different interpretation. The war was not an expression of God's free grace toward England; it represented, instead, his judgment on the nation. "I know that you are not such atheists, but you believe it is God that sends sickness, and famine, and war; and also that it is only sin that moves him to this indignation." In his view, Christians had been reluctant to reprove their neighbors for their drunkenness, swearing, worldliness, and ignorance, so God had acted to speak his own judgment on such behavior. "Guns and cannons speak against sin in England, because the inhabitants would not speak."[12]

In sum, Owen saw the war as a blessing from God, while Baxter viewed it as God's judgment on a sinful people. Same war, same side, but different worlds.

Reflections and Questions

So far we have followed the detail of our story only to 1646, when Owen preached to Parliament, and to 1647, when Baxter began to write his funeral sermon. They were a long way from meeting in person, but already a trajectory had been set, and when they finally encountered one another, each man found it

11 Owen, *Free Mercy*, in Owen, *Works*, 8:6.
12 Baxter, *Saints' Everlasting Rest* (1650), 495–96.

that much harder to understand where the other was coming from; mutual comprehension would be neither easy nor intuitive. Thanks to their divergent experiences of the civil war, they had come to see the same world in quite different terms. This fundamental misalignment would be challenging to overcome, especially when they might not even be aware of how their own and the other's prior experience continued to operate and influence them behind the scenes, as it were, of their conscious thoughts and actions.

We might pause here to reflect on the implications. One of the most powerful factors in this chapter is simply an accident of geography. If Baxter had lived in Essex and Owen in the Midlands, each man's perspective on England's civil war would have been completely different. A similar thing might be said of us. The effect may not be quite as pronounced in our life, or it could be even more pervasive, but we are all shaped by forces and experience beyond our ability fully (or even partially) to control—and that experience continues to have an effect whether we can recognize it or not. This is not to say that we are merely passive victims of the outside world: we are also shaped by the choices we ourselves have made. Baxter's life experience, for instance, would have been different if he had not chosen to sign up as an army chaplain. Similarly, our own choices, wise or foolish, constructive or destructive, continue to shape who we are and how we think about the world and others around us. Even so, we are, at a deep level, shaped by external forces over which we have little control. Understanding those forces and their effects, in ourselves and in others, is vital to mutual understanding. Otherwise, we are left in mutual incomprehension. We simply fail to appreciate or at least understand the other person. As you wrestle with these ideas, you might ponder the following questions.

1. Do you agree that each individual is profoundly shaped by factors largely outside his or her control? If so, why? And why does that matter?

2. Can you see how your own perspective has been shaped by factors beyond your control? As you think about this more carefully, have any of those external forces had an impact that, until now, you have not perceived or thought about? What has been the effect of those outside forces?

3. In what ways would it be helpful to look at others as having been shaped by the same sort of external forces? How might that change the way we perceive any differences between them and us?

4. Is it important to understand the perspective of the other person? If so, why does it matter? What kinds of qualities do we need in order to understand how others see the world from their point of view?

5. How much freedom do you think individuals have in choosing their perspective? What is the balance between intentionality and choice, on the one hand, and the dominance of those external forces, on the other? How could you shift the balance in your own life more toward intentionality and choice?

3

Personality

THE ISSUES THAT TRIGGER disagreement are usually obvious. At least they seem obvious. Those issues get debated, and positions soften or harden as the participants focus on the issues they believe to be at stake in any controversy. But what if more is at work than just those presenting issues? The difficulties between John Owen and Richard Baxter represented, as much as anything else, a personality clash. This is one more reason why the two men were never going to mesh easily. Not just their differing experiences of the civil war but their contrasting personalities would make mutual understanding much more difficult and disagreement much more likely, well before they had written or spoken a single word to each other. If we focus only on their disagreements over theological issues, we will miss the subtle but powerful impact of their experience and personality.

The brief story laid out in this chapter should be enough for us to see how their differences in personality might prove to be excruciating if they were played out (as indeed they were) in circumstances that served only to accentuate them. This is a deeply human story, and both Baxter and Owen come across as all too human. While it is fascinating to dissect their personalities, we might well reflect on our own and the extent to which personality plays a part in our conflicts or in the disagreements of those around us.

Owen's Personality

The problem with describing Owen's personality is that it is so very hard to find evidence for what he was like. He wrote no autobiography and left behind precious few personal documents. In general, all we have are his books. In this sense, they *are* his personality, but they give little away. In more than eighty publications, the only mention of his immediate family is a fleeting description of his father. He had eleven children, but only one lived into adulthood, and even she died before he did. Yet there is no mention of any of them in his writings. In this he could hardly be more different from Baxter, who left behind hundreds of letters and mountains of unpublished papers, and who demonstrated no reluctance to give himself away in his published work, sometimes (by seventeenth-century standards) in surprising and excruciating detail. Where it is hard to avoid Baxter, it is just as hard to find Owen. He directly contrasted himself with Baxter when he explained that the world was hardly likely to be interested in hearing about his personal life, so, entirely unlike Baxter, he firmly declined "to acquaint them with when I am well and when I am sick; what sin I have mortified most; what books I have read; how I have studied; how I go, and walk, and look."[1]

---

1   John Owen, *Of the Death of Christ and of Justification* (London, 1655), in *The Works of John Owen*, ed. William H. Goold, 16 vols. (1850–1853; repr., Edinburgh: Banner of Truth, 1983), 2:594.

If only he had. The result of his reticence, in the words of one historian, is that "Owen as a man, as a human being, still remains an elusive character."[2] So if we are to reconstruct his personality, we will have to interpret his actions, and this means frequently relying on those observing him, many of whom were critical. This approach, then, yields only a partial account of the man, but it is more than enough to help us understand why he would find Baxter so desperately hard to get along with.

For all that we do not know about Owen, one thing is clear: he possessed an ability to advance his career. Dedicating his first book, *A Display of Arminianism*, to the Committee for Religion in the House of Lords seems to have been a deft move, earning him a position in parish ministry soon afterward. The first invitation to preach to Parliament in April 1646 came about through a friend, Thomas Westrow, a member of Parliament. It might be seen as an early demonstration of Owen's ability to network, and he was not without ambition. It was about this time that he moved on (and up) to the larger parish of Coggeshall. In 1648, during a brief outbreak of renewed civil war, Colchester lay under siege. Owen's proximity brought him into contact with influential figures in the parliamentary cause and with other leading men in local and national politics. From there, his range of contacts extended considerably; Owen quickly accrued new responsibilities and prominence.

There is no better evidence of Owen's new standing than a second invitation to preach to Parliament on January 31, 1649, the day after the execution of King Charles I. Owen's sermon

---

2   Peter Toon, *God's Statesman: The Life and Work of John Owen* (Grand Rapids, MI: Zondervan, 1971), 176.

was not especially triumphalist, nor did it even mention Charles's execution specifically, but there could be no doubting his approval of events and the new regime's confidence in him to represent its voice. On April 19, 1649, he preached his third sermon to Parliament. This time, the audience included Oliver Cromwell, well on his way to becoming the most important political patron of all. A few days after the sermon, Owen called on the army leader Thomas Fairfax to pay his respects. While waiting to see him, Cromwell also arrived and, seeing Owen, crossed the room to lay a hand on his shoulder: "Sir, you are the person I must be acquainted with." Owen's reply was suitably demurring: "That will be much more to my advantage than yours." Cromwell responded, "We shall soon see that."[3] The awareness of patronage; the mutual balancing of favor, advantage, and service; and Owen's perfectly weighted reply all speak of his ease within the political rhythms of the day and further demonstrate his pursuit of influence, which quickly arrived. Cromwell invited him to serve as one of his chaplains in his campaign to suppress the long-standing rebellion in Ireland and, once that was achieved, in his campaign in Scotland to prevent the return of Charles II. Owen ceased his service as a chaplain to Cromwell in July 1651, but he continued to serve as chaplain to the Council of State through regular preaching that furthered his reputation. He has been called the "unofficial preacher-in-chief" of the new regime,[4] and he had become an

---

3   John Asty, "Memoirs of the Life of John Owen," in *A Complete Collection of the Sermons of the Reverend and Learned John Owen.* [. . .] *And to the Whole Are Prefixed Memoirs of His Life*, ed. John Asty (London: John Clark, 1721), 9.

4   Christopher Hill, *The Experience of Defeat: Milton and Some Contemporaries* (London: Bookmarks, 1984), 165.

essential member of the small team of ministers now well placed to influence religious policy. It is not far wrong to think of him as the architect of the Cromwellian church.

In 1651 Owen returned to his former university, this time as dean of Christ Church. In the following year, Cromwell nominated him vice-chancellor. From that position, he energetically set about to reform the university. But it was a battle, and how Owen engaged in that battle says something about his personality. One story is particularly revealing. Owen mounted a long and unsuccessful campaign against academic regalia—those gowns, hoods, and vestments that marked out the status of scholars. He viewed them as a relic of England's superstitious, Roman Catholic past, and he refused to wear them himself. Getting others to stop wearing them was another matter, even with all the powers of vice-chancellor.

In 1655 Owen unexpectedly summoned the academic staff to a meeting on the afternoon of Christmas Day, when few members could be present and he was much more likely to get his way. Which he did. The small number present voted to remove all statutes that required the wearing of regalia. It was a victory, then, though a short-lived one, since the next meeting overturned the decision. At a subsequent meeting, Owen declared that he had no more business to propose that day, waited for enough members to leave, then allowed another vote to permit those who wished to refrain from wearing regalia to do so. At a further meeting, he bundled several reforms, including the abolition of regalia, into one vote. The members were allowed no debate, they had only just seen the wording on which they were to vote, and they were required to vote on the whole package—it was all or nothing. Furthermore, in a highly unusual move, Owen wanted the members physically to divide into two groups, yea or nay, presumably to put more pressure on those inclined to vote against the measures. But they refused to obey his instruction. He then declared that the vote had passed without even seeing the results. In fact, the vote had failed, but the next day he asked for the record to show that it had passed. This request was refused.

Foiled and frustrated, he tried to achieve his aims through the Visitors, a group established to provide outside scrutiny of the university. But that did not work either. The Visitors were too evenly divided on this issue and in any case uncertain whether they had the power to amend the university's statutes. Faced with their reluctance, Owen, to the astonishment of his colleagues, headed to London. There he received no support at all from Cromwell. All this reveals his relentless determination to get his way, even by dubious means, but by 1657 the political tide was turning, and he lost his role of vice-chancellor. Despite his many other effective reforms, the wearing of regalia carried on unassailed.

This is only the briefest sketch of Owen's character, but it is still revealing in several ways. First, he was a political player, if not always successful. According to one contemporary, he was "politically addicted."[5] Today we might call him a "political animal." He was a born natural, possessed of the passion, insight, and skill necessary for political effectiveness. He was, according to his friend and early biographer John Asty, "well acquainted with men and things, and would give a shrewd guess at a man's temper and designs upon his first acquaintance."[6] If his preaching

5 John Goodwin to Sarah Goodwin, October 24, 1663, State Papers, National Archives, London, 29.82.39.
6 Asty, "Memoirs of the Life of John Owen," 34.

is anything to go by, he was eloquent and persuasive. According to another contemporary, "He had a very graceful behaviour in the pulpit, an eloquent elocution, a winning and insinuating deportment and could, by the persuasion of his oratory, move and win the affections of his admiring auditory almost as he pleased."[7] He seemed instinctively to understand the system of patronage, making his way up through local politics in Essex with ease and quickly breaking into national prominence, forming a bond with the man who would become his most powerful individual patron. His interaction with Cromwell in their first meeting represents an adept performance in the rhythms of deference and power. Later evidence at Oxford shows how Owen could trade on his close proximity to Cromwell to advance his program of reform.

He also possessed a pronounced streak of personal ambition. Asty said that he was "naturally of an aspiring mind, affecting popular applause, and very desirous of honour and preferment."[8] He could be touchy when it came to slights on his authority, and he was not a man to be contradicted. In the year after his death, an anonymous admirer vindicated him from the criticism of, as it happens, Richard Baxter. Near the end of the work, the author was prepared to offer a candid assessment. Owen "was indeed sometimes a little impatient of contradiction," and he was quite content to receive "honour, and respects from others."[9] In other words, he did not take kindly to having his will thwarted or to

7   Anthony Wood, *Athenae Oxonienses: An Exact History of all the Writers and Bishops who have had their Education in the* [. . .] *University of Oxford, from* [. . .] *1500 to the Author's Death in November 1695* [. . .], 2nd ed. (London: Knaplock, Midwinter and Tonson, 1721), 2:741.
8   Asty, "Memoirs of the Life of John Owen," 3.
9   *A Vindication of the Late Reverend and Learned John Owen* (London, 1684), 38.

being treated with less respect than he felt he deserved. He also exhibited a ruthless determination to achieve his desired ends, even if that meant overlooking proper procedure, and he reacted angrily when he did not get his way. Several of his contemporaries (both friends and opponents) commented on his tendency to respond with anger when others stood in his way. When he was removed as vice-chancellor in 1657, one acquaintance observed that "he cannot well digest a private life, but seems to be angry, at I know not what."[10] And when he did not get his way, he responded not just with anger but with a pattern of threats and withdrawal.

Admittedly, it is difficult to square this impression of Owen with his reputation as a towering theologian. We expect such figures to be above the foibles of mere human temperament, but they never are. This is also a most unflattering picture. It would certainly be possible to offer a more rounded and generous account; this is not the whole of the man. But it does explain something. If this is Owen's personality, what other type of personality would be likely to rub him the wrong way? Who would he find particularly grating and abrasive? The answer is someone who did not demonstrate proper deference, who lacked Owen's deft political facility, who blurted out the truth as he saw it with little regard for the feelings of others, who had his own implacable views, and who stood in Owen's way to oppose his every move. Someone, in other words, a lot like Richard Baxter.

Baxter's Personality

Unlike Owen, Baxter did write an autobiography, a long one, and almost the first thing he tells us is what happened soon after

---

10 Thomas Lamplugh to unknown, December 1657, State Papers, National Archives, London, 18.158.58.

his birth: "I lived apart from my parents with my grandfather till I was near ten years of age, and then was taken home."[11] We do not know the reason behind this arrangement. Certainly, we have no cause to doubt that this was anything other than a loving environment, and it is dangerous to speculate about the psychology of a person who lived in a world so very far removed from our own. But we might well ponder the effect that this detachment from parental bonding had on the formation of Baxter's temperament and personality. These days, we are well aware of how our brains are wired before we are three years old in ways that endure for the rest of our lives. It is just possible, though far from certain, that this early intervention contributed to a pattern of singular detachment that we see throughout Baxter's life.

We might also observe that he was an only child. Thus, he was never engaged in the kind of compromise and rough trading that must go on among siblings. He lacked the opportunity a larger family presented to develop skills in negotiation or empathy. He had his own way, with no near rival to contradict him. (We might bear in mind that Owen was, in contrast, the second of at least six children. This aspect of his upbringing conceivably contributed to his later skills in negotiating and networking.) When William Bates preached Baxter's funeral sermon, he recalled that as a little boy, "if he heard other children in play speak profane words, he would reprove them."[12] This seems a remarkable trait in one so young. We are told that it pleased his elders, but it could hardly have delighted his playmates. When Baxter returned to his parents,

---

11   Richard Baxter, *Reliquiae Baxterianae, or, Mr. Richard Baxter's Narrative of the Most Memorable Passages of His Life and Times*, ed. Matthew Sylvester (London, 1696), 1:1.

12   William Bates, *A Funeral Sermon for Richard Baxter*, 2nd ed. (London, 1692), 87.

he experienced a family culture isolated in its Puritan ways from the surrounding community. His father occasionally reproved "drunkards and swearers" and was roundly abused. Baxter and his parents could hardly hear their Psalms and Scriptures as they read the Bible on a Sunday afternoon, owing to "the great disturbance of the drum and pipe and noise in the Street!"[13] He was also unmarried, at least until his late forties, and he never had children. So he missed once more the opportunity for family life to rub off the rough edges of his character.

Not only that, Baxter never went to university, which was highly unusual for those who made their way into pastoral ministry. The point is that he was self-taught. University introduced young men to a network of fellow students who often became friends for life. It was above all a community. Students created valuable networks of enduring alliances. Teachers shaped minds. The academic art of disputation, arguing different sides of debated questions, disciplined students in how to think and how to make an argument, which inevitably refined their own thinking as a result. Baxter missed all this. He came to his views, in the main, by reading. He remained a voracious consumer of books his whole life long. It is a commendable practice, but by definition, one reads in isolation and on one's own, and books do not argue back.

All this helps explain the enduring irony of Baxter's life: he genuinely desired nothing more than to cultivate peace and unity, but his style and temperament regularly caused offense and generated conflict. Both friend and foe alike observed his tendency to come across as magisterial, haughty, arrogant, impervious to

---

13 Baxter, *Reliquiae Baxterianae*, 1:2–3.

correction, blind to his own weakness, incapable of self-doubt, and personally disdainful of others. For example, John Humfrey, a man who worked alongside Baxter in several of his aims, was prepared to speak honest words to a friend: "The thing in your writings which seems most grating is that you seem to be sometimes too dogmatic and confident," while "a few mollifying words and submission will take better."[14] This advice was wasted on Baxter, and three years later Humfrey had to repeat it. Others were now observing what he had already pointed out, and Baxter was doing himself no favors by persisting in a style "so violent, eager, sour, from the very first."[15]

Baxter was not unaware of the problem. In his reply to Humfrey, he explained, "I do not feel any passion or distaste against my brethren any more when I speak so keenly than at other times, but it is my natural temper to be earnest in speech, and when I write against an error, I am ready to think I should lay open the worst of it." His words may have seemed overly sharp at times, but his heart was not heated, nor did he intend to offend. But he added, "When I dispute against a sin or error, I should call it by its own name, and tell men truly what it is." The result, he said, was that "I often go further than I should, not well considering how grating and provoking some truths are to those that are dishonoured by them."[16] A year later he explained things more simply to another friend and fellow minister, Abraham

14 John Humfrey to Richard Baxter, May 11, 1654, Baxter Correspondence, Dr. Williams's Library, vol. 1, fol. 193v.

15 John Humfrey to Richard Baxter, ca. autumn 1657, Baxter Correspondence, Dr. Williams's Library, vol. 1, fol. 197.

16 Richard Baxter to John Humfrey, March 13, 1658, Baxter Correspondence, Dr. Williams's Library, vol. 1, fol. 203.

Pinchbecke: "I confess by the power of truth (if I mistake not) and an estimation of its interest above any other, I am strongly provoked to blab out anything that I do confidently think to be true and weighty."[17] These words suggest that Baxter had a degree of self-understanding, but in general, he was much more likely to lay the blame elsewhere, on those who could not bear any reproach with humility and graciousness. He continued to write as if he were in sole possession of the truth, without any hint of self-doubt.

This quality might be charitably described as a lack of empathy. He was too self-absorbed, too sure that he was right and others were wrong, too firmly convinced that the truth mattered above anyone's personal feelings to be overly concerned with the effect his words or actions might have on others. It makes some sense of the stubborn determination with which he held his own opinions. As he explained to a shrewd, supportive correspondent, Peter Ince, "I am as unapt to yield up my understanding to any man's and go upon trust, as most men that ever yet I was acquainted with." More to the point, he acknowledged, "I am more faulty in being too tenacious of my opinions (I think) than in being too mutable."[18] Indeed. His admission helps account for his tendency to be too severe in his writing style and to cause offense where he never discerned that any was intended or possible. One of the most significant effects of that propensity was to make him entirely unsuited to the practice of politics. "Though I offend,

---

17 Richard Baxter to Abraham Pinchbecke, October 12, 1658, Baxter Correspondence, Dr. Williams's Library, vol. 4, fol. 56.

18 Richard Baxter to Peter Ince, November 21, 1653, Baxter Correspondence, Dr. Williams's Library, vol. 1, fols. 11, 11v.

I must say that which cannot be hid."[19] For those who did not share his opinions, then, he was generally going to be a hard man to work with.

Reflections and Questions

After these two brief portraits, the contrast between the two men should be obvious. Owen was a political player with a deft political touch; Baxter most decidedly was not. Owen was a man who expected deference from those around him, who was "impatient of contradiction," who bristled at every slight, and who tended toward anger when his way was thwarted; Baxter was, by his own admission, inclined to "blab out" the truth as he saw it, "too tenacious of [his] opinions," and prone to saying too much, "not well considering how grating and provoking some truths are to those that are dishonoured by them." Owen was easily exasperated; Baxter was simply exasperating. The combination could hardly be more challenging, and we can now see the problem all too clearly. When these two personalities finally came into direct contact, the result was never going to be pretty.

At this point, we should remind ourselves of their enormous positive contribution, not least in their effective preaching and pastoral ministry and their many books that have been a blessing, a gift, and a fitting challenge to innumerable readers right down to the present day. It is unfortunate that this chapter has emphasized only the negative qualities of their personalities, but it has taught us a lesson in human frailty, weakness, brokenness, and fallenness, a condition in which we all share, if in very different ways.

19 Richard Baxter, *Richard Baxter's Confession of His Faith* (London, 1654), preface, sig. d4v.

Human fallibility cannot help but show up in our relationships. When disagreement breaks out, it is natural enough to focus our attention on the particular issues that have provoked it, but behind those issues, it may be that personality is doing a lot of the work in generating the disagreement. Dynamics of personality may require a response as much as the issues do. Vocal disagreements that seem on the surface to be merely theological (to choose one common trigger of disagreement) may be much more substantially the product of clashing personalities. Recognizing that factor is surely an essential requirement in resolving the conflict. For that reason, the place of personality when Christians disagree is well worth pondering.

1. Why is it that even sincere, faithful, godly Christians who genuinely seek to serve God and others can also demonstrate profound flaws that damage those around them? Should we just accept that reality, or should we challenge it?

2. How does your personality manifest itself when you are involved in conflict? Are you anything like Baxter or Owen? Is there anything in their story for you to pay attention to?

3. Can you think of a disagreement you have seen or been a part of that, on reflection, was more about a difference of personality than it was about the particular issues that seemed to provoke it? How does it help to distinguish the personalities involved from the issues at stake?

4. How might our response to discord change if we were to recognize the dimension of personality? What might we do differently to manage conflict when we seek to understand the people involved and the way their personalities are being expressed?

4

Theology

IT SEEMS ALMOST INEVITABLE that theology is involved when Christians disagree. They may fall out over explicit differences in doctrine, or they may differ over how theology is worked out in practice. Usually each side in a disagreement bolsters its position by appeals to the Bible. Theology does truly matter. But as we have seen, so does biography. It is impossible to separate how we think from what we have experienced; the waters are muddied.

When Richard Baxter and John Owen finally came into contact, they disagreed over soteriology, the doctrine of salvation, and this involved a cluster of related questions. In salvation, what is the place of God's choice and election, on the one hand, and our free will and moral responsibility, on the other? How much of the work is God's, and how much, if any, is ours? What did the apostle Paul mean when he wrote, "For by grace you have been saved through faith. And this is not your own doing; it is the gift of God, not a result of works" (Eph. 2:8–9)? When Christ died on the cross for our sins, for whom did he die? Was his death effective for the whole world or only for the elect? Did he pay the exact price for our sins, literally taking the place of each of the elect, or was his sacrifice more general and representative? Some of these kinds of soteriological questions remain relevant and significant today. But Owen and Baxter lived in a different age, so we might no longer ask quite the same questions they asked or ask them in the same way they did—and some of their questions may seem extremely technical to us. But even if we struggle to understand the complexities of their debate, the point to highlight here is that they gave different answers to all these questions in large part because each was driven by a different set of concerns.

Baxter's Theology of Salvation

Baxter's life took a notably new turn when he visited his friends in the army after the battle of Naseby in June 1645. It seems they had succumbed to a theological variant known as antinomianism. "No sooner was this doctrine received," he lamented, than it produced a "sudden looseness of their lives, answering their loose, ungospel-like doctrine."[1] It seems they were living as if their sin did not matter. Worse still, this disturbing theology was taking hold in the army and thus "spread among those who were likely to spread it through the land."[2] This is what provoked him to enlist as an army chaplain, in the hope of containing this spiritual disease.

---

1 Richard Baxter, *The Right Method for a Settled Peace of Conscience, and Spiritual Comfort* (London, 1653), 155.
2 Richard Baxter to Francis Tallents, January 7, 1656, Baxter Correspondence, Dr. Williams's Library, vol. 2, fol. 172v.

"Antinomian" literally means "against the law" (*nomos* is the Greek word for "law"). Indeed, some antinomians could argue that the moral law did not apply to them. They were beyond the reach of sin, and they could live exactly as they pleased. Others did not go nearly so far. In their case, "antinomian" served as a label of abuse. With just this one word, an opponent could be summarily categorized and dismissed, even if that person upheld the duty of the believer to live a godly life and observe the moral law. These "antinomians" looked back a century earlier to Martin Luther and a core belief of the Protestant Reformation: salvation by grace alone through faith alone. Antinomians took that literally and without qualification. Salvation was all of God and nothing of us. Salvation rested on free grace in Christ, not on our obedience, repentance, or perseverance. We can easily see how such thinking could lead to abuse: perhaps it did not matter at all how a believer lived.

The curious fact is that Baxter himself was initially sympathetic to many of the elements of antinomian theology. He later recalled how he "remained long in the borders of antinomianism, which I very narrowly escaped."[3] Perhaps at Naseby he glimpsed for the first time the danger of the very doctrines he then upheld. Even so, he later confessed that he had to be "cudgelled" to the truth "before [he] would admit it to [him]self."[4] He added, "I resisted the light as long as I was able."[5] It is possible that as he spent the next two years debating points of doctrine, he was arguing against

---

3 Richard Baxter, *Aphorisms of Justification* (London, 1649), appendix, 163.
4 Richard Baxter to John Warren, September 11, 1649, Baxter Correspondence, Dr. Williams's Library, vol. 6, fol. 96.
5 Baxter, *Aphorisms of Justification*, 291.

himself as much as the soldiers. He may have wanted to hold on to his previous soteriological convictions, but he could not ignore the ways in which those convictions freed those around him to abuse God's grace. This introduced a tension that needed resolution. He required a new theological system, one that retained some core convictions, jettisoned errant ideas, and secured human moral responsibility in salvation.

Illumination arrived in a dazzling flash of insight. It happened while Baxter was recuperating from his near-death experience in February 1647. As he was writing his funeral sermon, he wrestled with Matthew 25: "I seriously set myself to understand" this chapter, in which Christ judges the "sheep" and the "goats" on the basis of their works. "I found so great difficulties as drove me to God again and again." And then the moment of insight: "Thereupon came great light that I could not resist, so that I solemnly profess that it was partly on my knees, and partly in diligent consideration of the naked text that I received the substance" of a new theology of salvation. This was the defining moment in Baxter's theological development. He never spoke of another occasion with more excitement. "An over-powering Light," he enthused, "suddenly gave me a clear apprehension of those things that I had often searched after before in vain. Whereupon I suddenly wrote down the bare propositions."[6] In a flash of insight, then, pounced on by divine revelation, everything finally fell into place.

His new system was the mirror image of antinomian doctrine as he understood it. In his view, antinomians centered their theology on what he called strict imputation. At the cross, Christ

---

6   Richard Baxter, *An Unsavoury Volume of Mr. John Crandon's Anatomized: or a Nosegay of the Choicest Flowers in that Garden* (London, 1654), 5.

died literally in the place of believers. He took on himself their sin; they received his righteousness. His perfect fulfillment of the moral law was imputed to the elect, as if they themselves had perfectly fulfilled the law. He paid the exact price for their sin: the exact price, not an approximation or a general equivalent but the precise amount necessary to cover every sin of the elect. As a result, the elect were justified in the eyes of God from the moment of Christ's death—or even from eternity. Such was the force of God's election and such was the fullness of Christ's substitution at the cross that the salvation of the elect was complete and secure before they were even born. Furthermore, antinomians believed that the gospel was a promise, not a law, and when Christ was involved in conversion, he acted not as a king or lord but only as a priest. Thus the new covenant had no conditions or requirements. All was passive on our part, not active. Faith was simply the opening of the eyes of the elect to what had always been true: they were already righteous in the sight of God. They did not need to believe, repent, and obey because Christ had done that perfectly for them. So secure was their salvation in Christ that perseverance became redundant. It has to be said that this was not an accurate representation of what many "antinomians" actually believed, but this construction, fair or otherwise, is exactly what Baxter reacted against.

His new system rested on two important distinctions. First, he differentiated between God's will as "Dominus" and God's will as "Rector."[7] As Dominus, God ordered everything according to his secret and insuperable will. Baxter called this God's "Will of

---

7 Baxter outlined these distinctions in his *Aphorisms of Justification*, 1–11.

Purpose," in which God ordered events as he saw fit. This "Will of Purpose" contained his secret decrees of predestination and election. It was absolute and unconditional, and so was God's promise of justification to the elect. He added to this God's "Will of Precept," or his "Legislative Will," which focused on duty. The promises made according to this will were conditional. This is where the gospel fitted in. It was a law that set forth conditions, demanded duty, and threatened death to those who did not obey.

Second, he distinguished between two types of righteousness. The first was a "legal righteousness," which required perfect obedience to the law. Christ provided this righteousness, which was imputed to believers. But to avail themselves of this legal righteousness, believers had to bring a righteousness of their own to meet the terms of the new covenant. He called this "evangelical righteousness": a sincere but imperfect performance of the gospel conditions, which included faith, repentance, and perseverance. In this way, he restricted imputation only to the old covenant, not the new. When Christ died on the cross, he provided an amount of equal value that God graciously accepted as adequate for the remission of sin, not the exact amount for every precise sin.

Salvation, therefore, was active on our part, not passive. "Our evangelical righteousness consists in our own actions of faith and gospel obedience."[8] Far from being completed before we were born, a one-off event in the far-distant past, salvation was progressive, lifelong, and required our own participation. He distinguished three stages of justification. Only the first occurred in this life, when the believer met the conditions of the gospel

---

8   Baxter, *Aphorisms of Justification*, 108.

covenant. The final two stages took place after death, when God could declare each believer finally and fully justified. Salvation was complete not from eternity but only after death.

Baxter denied that this amounted to a doctrine of works, though he was prepared to use the word "merit," even with its Roman Catholic overtones, because God had promised to reward our works even if they had no worth in themselves. He argued that this element of human participation and responsibility was only a mere "peppercorn" that took nothing away from what Christ achieved on the cross.[9] Those who were saved under God's absolute "Will of Purpose" would be exactly the same individuals who met the requirements of God's "Will of Precept." He was trying to hold on to God's infallible election of individual believers *and* retain a place for human moral responsibility, but the resulting system was highly idiosyncratic. One critic called it a "hodge-podge divinity,"[10] and it gained few admirers. It revealed his lack of university training and reflected that inclination in his temperament to stand on his own on an island of one. Even so, he held it fast. Broadly speaking, this remained his way of understanding salvation for the rest of his life.

In sum, Baxter had reversed his soteriology. Once near-antinomian, it was now anti-antinomian. Why did he do that? The most obvious answer is that he thought it through, sincerely and prayerfully ("partly on my knees") while reading his Bible ("and partly in diligent consideration of the naked text"). "I seriously set myself to understand"; "I found so great difficulties as drove me

---

9 Baxter, *Aphorisms of Justification*, 127.

10 Samuel Young, *Vindiciae Anti-Baxterianae, or, Some Animadversions of a Book Intituled Reliquiae Baxterianae* (London, 1696), 111.

to God again and again."[11] All this speaks of thought and effort to see things clearly and truly. But we might venture deeper to ask if more was going on than meets the eye. I would argue that Baxter was traumatized by his experience of the civil war. As we have seen, the mid-1640s were for him a deeply troubling and unsettling few years. By the middle of the decade, there were signs that Parliament's army was fighting not merely to force King Charles to negotiate but to remove him. His execution was still several years away and still unthinkable, but Baxter claimed to have seen the first inklings of that turn when he visited the army at Naseby. From there he made connections with antinomian doctrine. After all, if the antinomians denied that Christ was King, would it not also make sense to deny that Charles was king?

Thus, Baxter blamed the antinomians for the perversion of the English Civil War. In a revealing letter of 1651, he lamented that previous generations had only heard of antinomian doctrine; they had "not seen what practical birth they travailed with as we have done." Recent events had shown "that the actors do not take sincere obedience to be any condition of salvation, nor the receiving of Christ as Christ, that is, as their king and lord, to be justifying faith." They do not take "his Gospel to be a law, either to guide or judge them." And he mourned the results: "the groans, tears and blood of the godly, the scorn of the ungodly; the stumbling of the weak, the hardening of the wicked; the backsliding of some, the desperate blasphemies and profaneness of others; the sad desolations of Christ's churches; and the woeful scandal that has fallen on the Christian profession." These "are all the fruit

---

11 Baxter, *Unsavoury Volume*, 5.

of this Antinomian plant."[12] In a period of acute anxiety, Baxter had identified something that brought great reassurance: someone to blame. The antinomian served as "the other." By putting up boundaries around antinomian doctrine, he was ordering his world. The clue to this analysis is that his new soteriology was the precise inverse of antinomian doctrine as he understood it. It betrayed a dynamic he articulated only years later: "Because the Antinomians deny it, let us prove it."[13] I am not suggesting that Baxter's theology was simply the manifestation of his fears, but we cannot ignore the traumatic context in which it was born.

The result is that Baxter, whose temperament compelled him to speak against error wherever he saw it, could never leave antinomian doctrine alone. "My apprehensions of the danger of that doctrine, commonly known by the name of Antinomian, are such as will not suffer me to make light of it, or patiently to sit still in silence while the Gospel is subverted by it, and the souls of poor people enticed to damnation."[14] Such urgency drove him to oppose antinomian tendencies wherever and in whomever he discerned them—even in someone, to be more specific, like John Owen.

Owen's Theology of Salvation

As we saw in chapter 1, Owen's experience of the civil war was entirely different from Baxter's, but that does not mean that his life was without trauma. For Owen, that hardship happened

---

12 Richard Baxter to John Warren, September 11, 1651, Baxter Correspondence, Dr. Williams's Library, vol. 6, fol. 199v.

13 Richard Baxter, *Universal Redemption of Mankind, by the Lord Jesus Christ: Stated and Cleared by the Late Learned Mr. Richard Baxter*, ed. Joseph Read (London, 1694), 398.

14 Richard Baxter, *Richard Baxter's Confutation of a Dissertation for the Justification of Infidels* (London, 1654), apologetical preface, sig. LL1.

earlier, during the 1630s, and while Baxter's trauma operated in the external world around him, Owen's difficulties lay entirely in his own inner world. It would seem from the account of one of his early biographers, his friend John Asty, that Owen experienced some sort of life crisis after he left Oxford University in 1637. His previous plans and ambitions now in disarray, this move "threw him into a deep melancholy that continued in its extremity for a quarter of a year, during which time he avoided almost all manner of converse and very hardly could be induced to speak a word, and when he did speak, it was with such disorder as rendered him a wonder to many." It is difficult to know quite what to make of this secondhand account offered five decades after the original episode, but it seems that Owen experienced a particularly severe and intense period of depression. "Though his distress and melancholy did not remain in that violence, yet he was held under very great trouble of mind and grievous temptations for a long time." Indeed, "it was near five years before he attained a settled peace."[15]

His tranquility came about when he heard a sermon preached by an unnamed minister he had never met. The text was Matthew 8:26: "Why are you afraid, O you of little faith?" It seems that the "very reading of the words" jolted Owen out of his despondency, and as the sermon unfolded, "the minister raised and answered those very objections which Mr. Owen had commonly formed against himself." This offers a hint of the kind of message he heard that day, one that brought reassurance to a young man apparently

---

15 John Asty, "Memoirs of the Life of John Owen," in *A Complete Collection of the Sermons of the Reverend and Learned John Owen.* [. . .] *And to the Whole Are Prefixed Memoirs of His Life*, ed. John Asty (London: John Clark, 1721), 4.

doubting his own worth and anxious over his own salvation. It is not that what he heard was necessarily new thinking to Owen. Indeed, the remarkable thing about the minister's sermon is that he managed his objections "in the same method which Mr Owen had frequently done in his own mind."[16] Having those thoughts somehow confirmed by another's voice brought a lasting sense of peace and assurance.

About a year later Owen published *A Display of Arminianism*, which articulated the outlines of his own theology of salvation. Arminianism strongly emphasized human autonomy, responsibility, and free will in salvation. In Owen's view, the Arminians aimed "to clear human nature from the heavy imputation of being sinful, corrupted, wise to do evil but unable to do good"—exactly the kind of sinful tendencies that he may have discerned in his own soul and yet was powerless within himself to change.[17] They denied "the eternity and unchangeableness of God's decrees" along with the "all-governing" and "energetical, effectual power" of God to bring about their fulfillment.[18] For Owen, however, God was sovereignly powerful in salvation. Without violating human free will, God infallibly brought about the perfect salvation of all those individuals he had predestined for salvation in a series of decrees and covenants issued before the creation of the world.

---

16 "The Life of the Late Reverend and Learned John Owen," in *Seventeen Sermons Preached by the Late Reverend and Learned John Owen* (London, 1720), 1:10–11. For a full account of the story, see Crawford Gribben, *John Owen and English Puritanism: Experiences of Defeat*, Oxford Studies in Historical Theology (New York: Oxford University Press, 2016), 41–42.

17 John Owen, *A Display of Arminianism* (London, 1643), in *The Works of John Owen*, ed. William H. Goold, 16 vols. (1850–1853; repr., Edinburgh: Banner of Truth, 1983), 10:13.

18 Owen, *Display of Arminianism*, in Owen, *Works*, 10:12.

To suggest, as the Arminians did, that God's plans for salvation were contingent on each person's choice to respond rendered God ultimately impotent and powerless.

In 1648 Owen followed up this first work with a second, longer discussion of the theology of salvation, *The Death of Death in the Death of Christ.* One of the key questions he addressed was the nature of Christ's satisfaction on the cross. When Christ offered himself as a sacrifice for sin, thereby remitting the debt that sinners owed to God, did he pay the exact debt for the precise and particular sins of those individuals (by standing specifically in their place and bearing the exact punishment that was theirs), or did he make some general form of recompense that was not, in fact, precisely the same in nature but was graciously taken to be so by God? Owen argued that Christ paid the exact debt for sin. His conclusion here is an important element in his understanding of the order of salvation that begins with what he called the "covenant of redemption." This was the agreement between the Father and the Son to appoint the Son as a mediator, the one whom the Father would punish for the sin of those he had chosen to save. A subsequent covenant was the "covenant of grace."[19] This was the agreement God had made, in Christ, to save the elect, of whom there is a specific number. This covenant had conditions, but God had determined to fulfill those conditions in the elect. Thus, salvation was assured, grounded as it was in God's infallible decrees from eternity. It is easy to imagine, then, how this style of theology, preached by that unnamed minister, would have provided so much reassurance. Owen learned then, and he

---

19   See John Owen, *The Death of Death in the Death of Christ* (London, 1648), book 3, chap. 1, in Owen, *Works*, 10:236–40.

never forgot, that his salvation was utterly and infallibly secure not because of his own efforts but because of God's sovereignty, power, and resources to establish the salvation of his elect.

Baxter and Owen Side by Side

At the close of this part of their story, it is worth pointing out just how much Baxter and Owen held in common. Both distinguished between the secret and revealed will of God. Both talked of a covenant of redemption (though Baxter preferred to call it a decree) between the Father and the Son to save the elect. Both emphasized a willing human response. Both accepted that salvation entailed a lifetime of perseverance and evidence of faith. Both believed that the elect would infallibly persevere. In other words, we can see both men as Calvinists.

The trouble is that while they shared an enormous amount of common ground, they stood back-to-back, looking in opposite directions and subject to opposite fears. Owen worried about the Arminians: they would be aided by anyone who emphasized, as Baxter did, human response and responsibility. Baxter worried about the antinomians: they would be aided by anyone who emphasized, as Owen did, God's eternal decrees and the exact price for sin paid by Christ on the cross. These underlying fears made it extremely difficult for each man to see in the other the many points they held in common. Rather, each one saw the other as aiding and abetting the enemy.

Likewise, both men experienced trauma but each of a different kind. The source of Baxter's trauma lay in the external world; Owen's drama played out on the internal landscape of his soul. His battle with depression may have left him with a felt need to look outside himself for the resources in his own salvation. While the ruinous experience of the wars gave Baxter little confidence in the external world, Owen's troubles may have fortified him against placing any great confidence in his own internal capacities. Thus, their differing experiences infiltrated each one's theology of salvation: Baxter hammering away at human responsibility, Owen constantly arguing that the only merits that mattered were those of Christ alone. This is not to minimize theological discussion, particularly when it comes to salvation, but what I want to highlight is that the particular concerns of each man led them to focus on different issues and talk past each other. Both felt the stakes were very high indeed—and for reasons that went beyond merely technical issues of theology. Theology was certainly part of their dispute but not the whole of it, and very human dynamics were at play in ways that they themselves were unable to recognize.

Reflections and Questions

In framing the theological disagreements between Owen and Baxter in this way, I am not suggesting that our theology is unimportant or that it is merely the product of our life experience, but it is inevitably shaped by it. People are not walking sets of ideas—pristine, changeless, and unaffected by the circumstances of life. We would do well to bear that in mind when disagreement breaks out over theological issues. We might ponder people's drivers and motivations, including our own. We might ask what buttons are being pushed that give particular issues the weight they appear to have.

We might also labor to hold the common ground, emphasizing the very great deal that holds us together and on which we do agree, rather than accentuating the differences. One dynamic we can observe in the experience of Baxter and Owen is that small differences become all the more excruciating the closer people are. Buddhists and Baptists, to choose random examples, may not ever come to blows, but disagreements among Baptists have the potential to become bitter indeed. If we can hold on to our common ground, perhaps the theological issues under debate can gain a more measured perspective.

Finally, a few of the questions Baxter and Owen disagreed over now seem strange and unimportant. This is a useful reminder that the issues that so energize us right now in our present moment might show themselves, in time, to have no importance at all. For that reason, we might hold them more lightly and be more reluctant to allow them to break the (too often) fragile unity of the people of God. With those thoughts in mind, you might ponder the following questions.

1. Can you see how your own life experience has shaped your theological point of view?

2. As you think of examples of theological controversy you have observed or been a part of, can you think of ways in which differing life stories and backgrounds have accentuated the differences?

3. What could we do to hold on to the common ground when controversy breaks out? Why is it so hard to do that? Why do the differences so easily dominate and distort our perspective?

4. If you had the opportunity, what advice would you give to Baxter and Owen about handling their theological disagreements?

.

5

Contact

WHEN WE FIRST ENCOUNTER another person, there is a great deal already in place that will shape the encounter for good or ill. Usually, the stakes are not that high, and any initial awkwardness can be set aside. But if the context in which we meet is itself fraught, there may be trouble. All this is illustrated in the story of how Richard Baxter and John Owen first came into contact. Before they even met, their contrasting experiences of the civil war, their opposing personalities and temperaments, and their differing theological concerns all conspired to make a mutual meeting of minds extremely difficult, if not impossible. But the context of their first contact could hardly have been worse. In response to a query from a friend, Baxter criticized Owen in his first publication, *Aphorisms of Justification*. Any criticism, especially public criticism, was never going to endear him to Owen. Thus their relationship stumbled right at the start, and from there it never recovered. As we watch how these events unfolded, we can see the way the dynamics we have observed in the previous three chapters now conspired to sour their relationship from the very beginning.

An Accidental Animosity

As we already know, Baxter very nearly died in February 1647, and during his recuperation, he took up his pen to write. This funeral sermon turned into something larger: *The Saints' Everlasting Rest*. And that in turn triggered something else again: his first published book, *Aphorisms of Justification* (an aphorism is a short, pithy statement of principle, though there is generally nothing short about Baxter's writings). Appearing in 1649, it contained all those "bare proposals" that had come to him in that life-changing moment of crisis and insight. The first 10 pages offered a clear statement of Calvinist doctrine. God promised infallibly to bring about the salvation of the elect—without any condition on their part—by choosing them and not others and by bestowing on them faith and perseverance. But in the remaining 325 pages Baxter set about constructing an elaborate set of boundaries designed to make very sure that none of his readers came to the conclusion that, in light of God's special distinguishing grace to the elect, they could live as they pleased. This sustained emphasis over hundreds of pages is hardly surprising. As he later explained, "I wrote that book especially against the Antinomians," those who argued that God did all in salvation with no meaningful place for our works or efforts.[1]

No doubt pleased with what he had put together, he sent the manuscript to an unnamed friend for his opinion. His friend

---

1 Richard Baxter, *Plain Scripture Proof of Infants' Church Membership and Baptism* (London, 1651), 191.

was not quite so pleased. He sent back a list of sixteen questions for Baxter to consider. In the last of them, he invited Baxter to ponder how his views aligned with Owen's in his latest book, *The Death of Death in the Death of Christ*, which had just come out (in February 1648). We can tell from Baxter's reply that he had not yet read Owen's book. He responded to his friend's questions with a 188-page appendix. Owen did not make an appearance until page 123, when Baxter finally came around to deal with his friend's sixteenth query. He found it an unpleasing task to have to respond to other writers who took a position different from his own, and he was also reluctant to point out the errors of authors who were otherwise "learned and godly," but he agreed to say something briefly.[2] Thus began his troubles with John Owen.

It was indeed a very narrow point of disagreement. Baxter explained that he could not "well understand Mr. Owen's mind," but it seemed that Owen had defended the notion that Christ paid the exact price for sin in place of the elect, not a generally equivalent amount that God graciously chose to accept.[3] Furthermore, Owen gave too much scope to "the laying of our sin on Christ" and the "imputation of his righteousness to us" in a method that sidestepped our own responsibilities and located the timing of that transaction at the cross.[4] Owen had used the illustration of a hostage lying in a distant prison who is freed at the moment when his ransom is paid, even if the news of that payment and his actual release took a long time to arrive. Baxter found this absurd. It was God, not the prisoner, who needed the

---

2 Richard Baxter, *Aphorisms of Justification* (London, 1649), appendix, 123–24.
3 Baxter, *Aphorisms of Justification*, appendix, 137.
4 Baxter, *Aphorisms of Justification*, appendix, 141.

knowledge of the ransom paid, and if the ransom had been paid at the time of Christ's death, there was nothing to stop God from bringing about the immediate release of the hostage.

Baxter had made no bones about his disagreement with Owen, but it has to be said that his tone was relatively measured. "It grieves me to see many of our ministers fight against Jesuits and Arminians with the Antinomians' weapons, as if our cause afforded no better; and so they run into the far worse extreme."[5] That is about as much as he said of Owen. He fought in a good cause but with the wrong weapons, and he risked running into a greater error than the one he was fighting against. In *Death of Death*, Owen looked rather too antinomian for Baxter's liking, though he did not accuse him directly.

Baxter did not quite know whom he had taken on, nor had he quite discerned the dangerous territory into which he had strayed. By 1649 Owen was a man on the rise, a man possessed of a temperament that did not look kindly on criticism, certainly not from an unknown upstart writing from the middle of nowhere. At this point, Owen was in Dublin, trying to put Trinity College on a better footing at the request of Oliver Cromwell, to whom he was now chaplain. He took time out of his work to put together a short reply to Baxter, which he finished in December 1649 and published early the following year. In that book (called *Of the Death of Christ*, not to be confused with his earlier book, *The Death of Death in the Death of Christ*), he recalled his hope that the civil wars—God's vindication of the gospel—had been enough to stop the spread of Arminian doctrine. Instead, "not

5 Baxter, *Aphorisms of Justification*, appendix, 164.

a few are attempting once more to renew the contest of sinful, guilty, defiled nature, against the sovereign distinguishing love and effectual grace of God."[6] These "not a few" now included Baxter. In response, Owen reaffirmed his view that the punishment Christ endured on the cross was precisely what the law required for each member of the elect, not some general representation, and he vehemently denied that he had ever argued for the justification of the elect from eternity or from the cross. "To have an opinion fastened on me which I never once received or intimated . . . is a little too harsh dealing." To be criticized now "as a patron of that opinion seems to me something uncouth."[7] He was deeply offended, and the language he used throughout his short reply made that very clear. Baxter had deliberately cast Owen's doctrine "into a crooked frame," and he had done so "with some passages of censure that might have been omitted without losing the least grace of his book or style."[8] Baxter had gotten off on the wrong foot, to say the least.

To understand what was going on at this point, we might borrow from the thinking of Joseph Caryl. He moved in similar circles to Owen and felt the burden of forging unity among committed believers. In 1652 he published a book called *The Moderator*, which sought to reconcile the differing parties within the English church. His opening analysis identified a breakdown in trust: "He that does not confide in his neighbours hinders them from confiding in him, and he that fears others creates in them a fear against

6 John Owen, *Of the Death of Christ* (1650), in *The Works of John Owen*, ed. William H. Goold, 16 vols. (1850–1853; repr., Edinburgh: Banner of Truth, 1983), 10:431.

7 Owen, *Of the Death of Christ*, in Owen, *Works*, 10:449.

8 Owen, *Of the Death of Christ*, in Owen, *Works*, 10:436.

himself." In this fashion, Baxter had inadvertently strayed into dangerous territory by critiquing Owen's work in the appendix to his *Aphorisms of Justification*. It was not an approach that was going to engender trust in Owen; instead, it produced unease and uncertainty. In his turn, Owen's response also did nothing to build trust and understanding. "For if I cannot bring my spirit to trust my neighbour," said Caryl, "how can I expect that his spirit should be brought to trust me? If I think that he does not trust me, I will readily suspect him. If I suspect him, I will arm myself to oppose him or weaken him lest he oppose me." Thus, "if I give way to these thoughts, I am at war with him in my heart and the only thing that can foster confidence in him, the affection of Christian love and generous sincerity, is lost between us."[9] By 1652, the year of Caryl's book, there was no sign at all of any mutual love and generosity between Owen and Baxter. Trust had already been lost.

Continued Conflict

In looking back on *Aphorisms of Justification* some years later, Baxter expressed some regret: "I meddled too forwardly with Dr. Owen, and one or two more that had written some passages too near Antinomianism."[10] He was young, he explained, and he assumed that others would receive criticism as easily as he could. He did not then understand that pointing out the errors

9   Joseph Caryl, *The Moderator: Endeavouring a Full Composure and Quiet Settlement of Those Many Differences Both in Doctrine and Discipline, Which Have So Long Disturbed the Peace and Welfare of This Common-Wealth* (London, 1652), 3.
10 Richard Baxter, *Reliquiae Baxterianae, or, Mr. Richard Baxter's Narrative of the Most Memorable Passages of His Life and Times*, ed. Matthew Sylvester (London, 1696), 1:107.

of others would only "provoke them more passionately to insist on what they once have said."[11] His encounter with Owen taught him that lesson the hard way, and he lapsed into uncharacteristic silence. In a moment of rare restraint, he chose not to reply to *Of the Death of Christ*.

He did not reply, that is, until 1655, when he published *Richard Baxter's Confession of His Faith*. He intended this book, nearly five hundred pages long, as an update and improvement on his *Aphorisms of Justification*. He engaged with Owen in a scattering of places in ways that were both brief and respectful (Owen was "the most sober and learned man that I know of, that writes this way"),[12] and he responded only because a matter of genuine importance was at stake ("Though I offend, I must say that which cannot be hid").[13] His most intense engagement came in the middle of the book, where he picked apart the second section in *Of the Death of Christ*, in which Owen had denied the charge of affirming justification from eternity and clarified his view of what had transpired at the cross for the elect. Here Baxter could quote Owen's own language that Christ had "merited on their behalf, yes, in their stead, they dying with him."[14] Such words sent a shudder down his spine: "Here is the heart of the whole controversy, and the root of many dangerous errors, I think very plainly subverting the Christian religion."[15] This was about as close as he could come to accusing Owen of antinomianism without actually doing so.

---

11 Baxter, *Reliquiae Baxterianae*, 1:107.

12 Richard Baxter, *Richard Baxter's Confession of His Faith* (London, 1655), 219.

13 Baxter, *Richard Baxter's Confession of His Faith*, preface, sig. d4v.

14 Baxter, *Richard Baxter's Confession of His Faith*, 266, quoting Owen, *Of the Death of Christ*, in Owen, *Works*, 10:468.

15 Baxter, *Richard Baxter's Confession of His Faith*, 266.

Once again, Owen was unlikely to take such criticism lying down, and his response appeared within months in the third of his books with a similar title. *Of the Death of Christ and of Justification* was a short appendix to his massive work defending an orthodox understanding of the gospel against the Socinians (who, we might recall, denied the Trinity and the deity of Christ). Owen's reply to Baxter may have been brief, but it was heated and pointed. By now he felt himself to have been grievously insulted. It is easy to read into his words a tone that is by turns offended, bitter, sarcastic, and bewildered. He repeated his earlier denials, criticized Baxter's arrogance and method, engaged with the latest provocation point by point, clarified the pertinent aspects of his theology of salvation, and amplified his previous cutting tone. His reply reveals him at his most devastating, using every means available to demolish Baxter: the placement of the text itself at the end of a book against the Socinians; visibly and uncharacteristically excessive Latin and Greek quotations; deft irony and, in places, sarcasm; and clear, defiant, forceful rejoinders. Owen placed all his learning and skill on show. He conveyed in very clear undertones that Baxter's efforts were not to be suffered.

For him, the problem was that Baxter just did not listen. If Owen had to carry on a debate, he would have preferred to do so, as he said, "with those who, understanding my meaning, will fairly, closely, and distinctly, debate the thing in difference, without insisting on words and expressions to no purpose."[16] Baxter did not. His method was to manipulate Owen's words to fit his argument. Essentially,

---

16 Owen, *Of the Death of Christ and of Justification* (Oxford, 1655), in *The Works of John Owen*, ed. William H. Goold, 16 vols. (1850–1853; repr., Edinburgh: Banner of Truth, 1983), 12:605.

Owen was saying that Baxter saw too much of what he wanted to see and too much that reflected Baxter's own suppositions. He did not show the discipline (or the moral rectitude) of dealing with what Owen actually said and intended. "I am enrolled into the troop of Antinomians," he complained.[17] Baxter had cast "the aspersion of me for an Antinomian."[18] Owen was outraged. Baxter's writings were full of "pride and passion, magisterial insolence, pharisaical, supercilious self-conceitedness, contempt of others, and everything that is contrary to the rule whereby I ought to walk."[19] All this amounted to a remarkably personal, bitter, and scathing rebuke.

And Baxter felt it. He did not reply at length, but he did reply in a work that he began to write immediately yet that did not appear in print until 1657. He complained that he had been personally attacked, "voluminously slandered," and roundly criticized as "hypo-critically proud."[20] Instead of understanding, he had received from Owen "ingenious malice."[21] Owen was the contradictory voice of Shimei, sent by God to do David good (2 Sam. 16:5–14) and "a messenger of Satan to harass" him and keep him humble (2 Cor. 12:7).[22] But Baxter continued to argue that Owen had promoted the doctrine of justification from eternity, even though Owen had

---

17 Owen, *Of the Death of Christ and of Justification*, in Owen, *Works*, 12:601.

18 Owen, *Of the Death of Christ and of Justification*, in Owen, *Works*, 12:592.

19 Owen, *Of the Death of Christ and of Justification*, in Owen, *Works*, 12:615.

20 Richard Baxter, *Certain Disputations of Right to the Sacraments, and the True Nature of Visible Christianity* (London, 1657), 484.

21 Baxter, *Certain Disputations*, 487.

22 Baxter, *Certain Disputations*, 486. Shimei pelted King David with stones and curses as he fled Jerusalem during his son Absalom's revolt; David accepted Shimei's curses as from the Lord (2 Sam. 16:5–14). To keep the apostle Paul from becoming proud over his visions and revelations, he says, "A thorn was given me in the flesh, a messenger of Satan to harass me, to keep me from becoming conceited" (2 Cor. 12:7).

insisted time and time again that he did not, and then he claimed that Owen had conceded his position. "When a bad cause is disowned, I have the thing that I intended." This statement could only have infuriated Owen: How could he disown a cause that he had never owned in the first place? Baxter claimed a victory where there was none. And so we come to what Baxter called "the displeasure of the Reconciled," the state in which he now viewed their relationship. Owen had disavowed his bad cause, and the two men were in broad, if heated, agreement: "And though it be very angrily that we agree, and close with somewhat a sharp collision, yet it is well that we agree."[23] Angry agreement: that is the best he could hope for and the most he could salvage from the wreckage of their relationship.

Reflections and Questions

Baxter and Owen had at last come to blows, in print at least, and it is reasonably easy to understand how and why that happened. Baxter, traumatized by the civil wars, apprehensive of the looseness of antinomian doctrine, and afflicted with a personality that compelled him to speak the truth regardless of the cost in personal relationships, veered into Owen's path. Owen, of course, anxious about the peril of Arminianism and burdened with a personality that bristled at any slight, refused to let Baxter's comments pass on by. Thus we see at work deep-seated dynamics that reveal much about the two men.

But this disastrous beginning was also accidental. It just so happened that Baxter sent his manuscript to a friend. It just so happened that his friend had recently read Owen's latest

---

23 Baxter, *Certain Disputations*, 483.

book and wondered what Baxter would make of it. So he added a discussion of Owen at the end of his sixteen queries. If the list had ended at fifteen, this chapter would never have been written, and the relationship between Owen and Baxter, when it did begin to form, may have been given the chance to settle. Any such relationship between them was never going to be easy, but perhaps, if they had come into contact in a more conducive context, each one might not have formed such a jaundiced impression of the other. Maybe they might have found a way to work together constructively, if not always amiably. But it was not to be. There were sixteen questions on that list, and when Baxter answered the final query, he set in motion events that would undo his relationship with Owen from the very beginning.

So it is with us. There are deep personal dynamics involved in any conflict, but they tend to be triggered by mundane events. Those events are contingent; they happen in one particular way and not another and with discernible effects as they work themselves out. Sometimes the results are excruciating. We cannot go back in time, but perhaps we can take a step back and choose to let some things go or at least see the actions of the other in the most generous light possible, not the most hostile. It helps, of course, if we can communicate directly and openly, but with Baxter in Kidderminster and Owen in Dublin, there was no hope of that. What we see instead is the power of the written word to inflame acrimony and misunderstanding. The fact that these words were published for all to see only raised the stakes and made any sort of reconciliation that much harder. Pride and ego came into play, rather than humility, kindness, and generosity. The damage had been done. By 1650 the written word had estranged two men who had not yet even met. We might ponder that as we think about our own day.

1. Think back over the way Baxter and Owen spoke to each other in print. How do their responses reveal the weaknesses in each one's personality? How does that illustrate the importance of understanding our own weakness, and those of others, when conflict occurs?

2. It did not help that Baxter and Owen aired their differences in print, making them both public and permanent. Can you see similarities with social media in our day, when people say things online that they would never say in person? Are there lessons to learn from the way these two men carried on their printed dispute as we navigate the challenges of social media? How important are civility and restraint in how we communicate with someone with whom we differ?

3. Even if we never make our concerns public, as Baxter and Owen did, one way to approach our differences with another person is to communicate those concerns in writing. Or we can talk to them face-to-face. What are the advantages and disadvantages of each approach? Do you think one method is generally to be preferred over the other? If so, why?

4. As we saw in the previous chapter, some of the particular theological issues that were so important to Baxter and

Owen might now seem foreign, trivial, and pedantic to us. Is it possible that the issues that animate controversy today can be equally the product of our own time and place and, taking a long view, are not important enough to divide over? Are the issues that so exercise us in fact peripheral? Are we being driven by those issues or by a concern for our own esteem or for the reputation of the group with whom we identify? How can we tell when an issue at stake is important enough for us to take a stand or not?

5. Plenty of verses in the New Testament call on us to seek unity and act lovingly, yet it seems those verses did little to shape the actions of Baxter and Owen. Why do you think that was? What got in the way? How would you balance the call to love with the need to protect the truth? Do you find one side of that balance easier than the other? If so, why, and how does it help to be aware of that?

6

Collision

IN THE PREVIOUS CHAPTER, you may have noticed that the printed exchange between John Owen and Richard Baxter in the middle of the 1650s carried a layer of vitriol that was absent from their first encounter when the decade began. In 1655, as we saw, Owen condemned Baxter's "pride and passion, magisterial insolence, pharisaical, supercilious self-conceitedness, and contempt of others."[1] In 1657 Baxter called Owen "a messenger of Satan to buffet me."[2] Clearly, something bad had happened to worsen their relationship: they had met in person for the first time.

So far this story has felt a little like watching two vehicles rapidly traveling toward each other along the same narrow, misty road. From our elevated perspective, we can calculate the trajectories.

---

1   John Owen, *Of the Death of Christ and of Justification*, in *The Works of John Owen*, ed. William H. Goold, 16 vols. (1850–1853; repr., Edinburgh: Banner of Truth, 1983), 12:615.

2   Richard Baxter, *Certain Disputations of Right to the Sacraments, and the True Nature of Visible Christianity* (London, 1657), 486.

We can see what is coming; the drivers cannot. We close our eyes and brace for impact. Likewise, the relationship between Baxter and Owen feels like an accident that was always going to happen. There were so many points of contrast that the two men were never going to mesh easily even in the best of circumstances, and when they did finally meet, in 1654, it was not the best of circumstances. Sadly, the context was one that exposed their differences with excruciating precision. Somehow it feels inevitable that the fundamental differences we have explored so far would lead them on to still other points of divergence. They also had rival visions for, of all things, church unity. Both men wanted it; they just disagreed on how best to achieve it. The irony is that working together on unity served to drive them further apart.

Baxter's Vision for Unity

When Baxter published his *Aphorisms of Justification* in 1649, he began it with a letter to the reader in which he condemned those who set themselves up to be "creed makers."[3] A creed is a statement of belief or doctrine. The earliest creeds were few and relatively short, but since the time of the Reformation a century earlier, confessions, a longer counterpart to creeds, had proliferated and become ever more elaborate. Anyone with eyes to see could observe that such confessions had done little to restore the unity of what had been one Western church. Instead, Baxter saw only increasing division and fragmentation. It seemed to him that such lengthy and intricate statements of faith served to hasten division among Christians, not remove it. He wondered if a believer from

---

3 Richard Baxter, *Aphorisms of Justification* (London, 1649), epistle to the reader, sig. a2v.

the early church who firmly held to the Apostles' Creed or the Nicene Creed would even be accepted as a Christian in this later, contentious, confession-ridden age. It was simply impossible for all Christians to find agreement in a lengthy formula expressed in merely human language. Instead, he believed that church unity should rest only on the one text that all Christians could agree on: the Bible. He called this idea "Scripture sufficiency." While it was permissible to have a confession as a test of faith, he was adamant that the language in that confession should derive only and exclusively from Scripture.

In some ways, it was a strange thought with which to begin his *Aphorisms*, a book that departed from the language of Scripture in so many of its key terms, but Scripture sufficiency was for Baxter a deep and consistent concern. That was not the case earlier in his life. He recalled a time when he measured Christians in too narrow a set of terms "and thus was involved in the guilt of faction."[4] His 1640s experience changed all that. The trauma of war left him yearning not only for order and godly living (threatened by the antinomians) but also for peace. He never wanted to go through anything like that ordeal ever again. Long-standing theological issues played a part in generating the war, and they could do so again. As he put it in a letter of 1670, England was "living in a Heart-War, and a Tongue-War, which are the sparks that usually kindle a Hand-War."[5] Words could kill! Weapons on the page

4 Richard Baxter, *Richard Baxter's Confession of His Faith* (London, 1655), preface to the reader, sig. D3v.
5 Richard Baxter to the Earl of Lauderdale, June 24, 1670, in Richard Baxter, *Reliquiae Baxterianae, or, Mr. Richard Baxter's Narrative of the Most Memorable Passages of His Life and Times*, ed. Matthew Sylvester (London, 1696), 3:77.

could too easily turn into weapons in our hands. After the 1640s, Baxter was a man desperate for peace and unity among Christians as far as practicably possible. "I am resolved," he said in 1658, "to speak for peace, while I have a tongue to speak, and to write for peace, while I have a hand to write, and to live to the church's peace, while I have an hour to live and am able to do anything that may promote it."[6] He really meant it.

But how could peace be best achieved? If elaborate confessions were not the answer, what was? Baxter advocated practice, not statements of principle or belief. He observed that his fellow Puritans essentially agreed on their practical aims even if they disagreed on narrow points of church doctrine. He first laid out his plan in the second edition of his *Saints' Everlasting Rest*, published in 1651. He identified four main parties within the community of godly, orthodox Christians (Congregationalist, Episcopalian, Erastian, and Presbyterian). He was convinced that the moderates in each of those four groups stood in essential agreement over what they thought churches, ministers, and believers should be doing in practice. Therefore, the solution to England's divided Christianity was, he said, for the moderates in all four parties "to come as near together as they possibly can in their principles; and where they cannot, yet to unite as far as may be in their practice, though on different principles; and where that cannot be, yet to agree on the most loving, peaceable course in the way of carrying on our different practices."[7] Baxter consistently advocated this course of

6 Richard Baxter, *The Grotian Religion Discovered, at the Invitation of Mr. Thomas Pierce in His Vindication, with a Preface Vindicating the Synod of Dort* (London, 1658), 6.

7 Richard Baxter, *The Saints' Everlasting Rest*, 2nd ed. (London, 1651), dedication of the whole, sig. a1v.

action throughout the 1650s, and he put it into practice in his own beloved parish.

Kidderminster experienced a reformation under Baxter's leadership and ministry. The town of around three to four thousand inhabitants was transformed from one in which godly families were a tiny minority to one in which such families predominated. It changed the character of the town. All this was mostly the fruit of Baxter's preaching and his dedicated, intentional, and demanding practice of pastoral ministry. He set aside two full days a week in which he and his assistant would meet for an hour with families to assess the condition of their Christian faith, thus meeting with every willing family in the parish over the course of a year. He conscientiously practiced confirmation, ensuring that those who came to an age of understanding genuinely understood the faith and made it their own. And he employed the instruction Jesus laid out in Matthew 18 to challenge sinners and excommunicate the impenitent. As a result, the town grew in visible godliness.

But Baxter did not do this work in isolation. He reached out to the ministers living nearby in Worcestershire, of whatever doctrinal persuasion. He formed the Worcestershire Association. In 1653 he and his fellow ministers published *Christian Concord: or The Agreement of the Associated Pastors and Churches of Worcestershire*. In it they resolved to practice effective church discipline, such as Baxter was doing in Kidderminster. In 1656 they followed this up with *The Agreement of Diverse Ministers of Christ in the County of Worcester*, in which they agreed to practice the routine of individual family visitation that Baxter had pioneered in his town. These ministers met together monthly to encourage each other and to discuss difficult cases of church discipline. The Worcestershire Association was Baxter's vision for church unity made real. Even if these ministers worked from different principles, they could agree on the practice of effective pastoral ministry.

Things nearly fell apart in 1653. By late 1652 the ministers in the association were close to agreement on the text of a shared confession of faith, but one sticking point remained. It is an essential part of Trinitarian orthodoxy that the Holy Spirit is God. The problem was that the Bible did not say that in plain terms; it was a truth one had to infer from more than ample evidence and indications throughout Scripture. Baxter would not budge on using only the exact language of Scripture in their shared confession, but that made it extremely difficult to convey the deity of the Holy Spirit. Not only that, England was now being haunted by the specter of the Socinians. At their most extreme, they viewed the Trinity as a later human construction overlaid on the Bible from outside. As we will see, they also argued for a "scriptural sufficiency" in language that was eerily close to that of Baxter. So at the very time when the deity of the Holy Spirit had to be affirmed in the clearest terms, Baxter could not bring himself to depart from the language of Scripture. He and his fellow ministers debated different variants at length, to no avail. They were stuck in an impasse.

At last, he sought advice from a credible outside figure of authority, John Dury, who had worked tirelessly to bring about unity among the various Protestant groups in Europe. Dury helped Baxter find a construction that worked for everyone: "I believe that God the Holy Ghost, the Spirit of the Father and Son, was sent from the Father by the Son, to inspire and guide . . . and to dwell and work in all that are drawn to believe . . ."[8] Thus the crisis was resolved, and the association moved on. But this shows just how delicate the project of unity was. Baxter nearly failed to find agreement with men who knew him well and wanted to work with him. It remained to be seen how he would get on negotiating with those who did not know him well or who viewed him with distrust.

Owen's Vision for Unity

In direct contrast to Baxter, Owen rather liked confessions of faith. For him, the basis for church unity was principles, not practice, mainly because it proved a handy way of protecting Congregationalists from the accusation of schism. They formed new congregations of "visible saints" to sit alongside (and rival) the traditional parish church. No one could say this was an act of schism if the basis of unity among all true believers was an intangible set of common doctrines rather than an institutional, visible structure. Furthermore, those doctrines holding all believers together in unity could only be those that were essential for salvation, not matters of secondary importance. If a person did not agree with all these essential doctrines, then he or she was not a genuine Christian.

As Owen explained in *Of Schism*, published in 1657, those necessary doctrines "are commonly called fundamentals, or first principles, which are justly argued by many to be clear, perspicuous, few, lying in an evident tendency to obedience." If the fundamentals were "savingly believed," a person was made "a member

8 Richard Baxter, *Christian Concord: or the Agreement of the Associated Pastors and Churches of Worcestershire* (London, 1653), profession, sig. C3.

of the church catholic invisible," and "the profession of those truths" incorporated a person "in the unity of the church visible."[9] Those congregations that adhered to the fundamentals would be tolerated by the state even if they differed on minor matters of practice such as church government. Thus the fundamentals of the faith could also be used to distinguish truly Christian groups from false, heretical ones. This was, he believed, the best means of attaining "peace and union among Christians."[10]

It was a nice idea, but it required two things. First, everyone had to agree on what was fundamental and what was not. Second, everyone had to agree on a form of words that accurately represented those fundamentals. This would be no easy task, but that did not discourage Owen from trying, and by the early 1650s, he was well placed to influence England's religious policy. On February 10, 1652, Owen, along with three other Congregationalist leaders, presented a petition to Parliament, which triggered the *Proposals for the Furtherance and Propagation of the Gospel in This Nation*. The *Proposals* represented the first-draft iteration of the fundamentals. In the end, though, they ran up against a political reality that never went away. Even if Owen and his fellow ministers devised an agreed-on list of the fundamentals, those doctrines had to receive parliamentary approval. For various reasons, that approval never came. So this first draft came to nothing, but it did not stop Owen from trying again.

In the meantime, Parliament gave Owen another weighty task. By the 1650s the Socinian threat was only growing in magnitude.

---

9 John Owen, *Of Schism: The True Nature of It Discovered and Considered* (London, 1657), in Owen, *Works*, 13:146.

10 Owen, *Of Schism*, in Owen, *Works*, 13:96.

Someone had to write the definitive work against their theology, and Owen was the man to do it. Through 1654 and into the following year, he labored away at a massive and truly monumental book, *Vindiciae Evangelicae, or, The Mystery of the Gospel Vindicated and Socinianism Examined*. It was 667 pages long and was published in 1655. It targeted particularly one of England's most notorious Socinians, John Biddle, while also engaging generally with other related thinkers. This is where Owen took aim at Baxter. At the end of the book, he attached his brief reply to Baxter's *Confession of His Faith*. This was a calculated placement. As we will soon see, Owen was worried that Baxter's theology served only to encourage the Socinians.

So Owen was writing that book in 1654 when he became involved in a renewed effort to formalize the fundamentals. England's new written constitution, the Instrument of Government (which created a form of government called the Protectorate), contained articles that embodied his view of toleration. When the First Protectorate Parliament met in September 1654, it quickly recognized in those articles the need to identify the fundamentals of the faith on which all could agree. It formed a subcommittee of around a dozen minister-theologians to prepare a list of the fundamentals for the approval of Parliament and the Lord Protector, Oliver Cromwell. This group began to meet on November 4 and carried on into December. Its membership is not entirely certain, but it comprised a balance of Presbyterians and Congregationalists, including several figures who had worked closely with Owen. One nominated member, Archbishop James Ussher of Armagh, Ireland, declined to take part, so another man was sent in his place. We do not know how Owen reacted when he first learned the name of that replacement, but he can hardly have relished the prospect of working with someone who had already proved such an irritant in print. Indeed, by then Baxter was on his way from Kidderminster to London. The two men were to meet at last.

The 1654 Subcommittee

What a moment that must have been when Baxter walked in the door of the Jerusalem Chamber at Westminster Abbey, when he and Owen first set eyes on each other and they exchanged greetings. It is worth pausing briefly to recall that they came into the same room with very different life experiences, opposing personalities, contrasting theological concerns, and a history of sniping at each other in print. Furthermore, as we have now learned, they arrived with differing agendas over the very purpose of the subcommittee in which they were both to play a part. How could this ever go well? The forces that had conditioned their lives up to this point now profoundly shaped their first encounter.

We cannot know how that moment passed, but we do know how things degenerated from there. Baxter gave a full account in his autobiography. It is, of course, a partial perspective that presents us with his side of the events. Even so, he unwittingly betrays his own blind spots and weaknesses. His recollections are both plausible and predictable, as each man behaved exactly as we might expect. It was Baxter's misfortune to arrive late and entirely characteristic of Owen (assuming he was chairing the subcommittee) not to wait for his appearance. From the beginning, Baxter was a very square peg in a very round hole. It would have taken only a short time for everyone to work that out because his position was simple and pure: he could not accept any formulation of authorized doctrine that went even one syllable beyond the words of Scripture. "We are framing a means of union, not of division," he said to them. "And though it grieves me to be offensive to my brethren, yet I would rather suffer anything in the world than be guilty of putting among our fundamentals one word that is not true."[11] This was an absolute position on which he would not compromise; it was a zero-sum game. As soon as that fact was made plain, the other ministers could do nothing except to adopt Baxter's stance or reject it, and they simply could not accept it. It would have had almost the same effect on the outcome and would have made more friends among the other participants if he had simply taken the next coach home. As it was, he stayed for the duration of the deliberations, acting as little more than a thorn in the side of most, if not all, of his fellow ministers—and of Owen in particular.

It is not that Baxter did not offer some constructive suggestions. He did. But they were untenable to almost all the other ministers. He suggested that the Apostles' Creed, the Lord's Prayer, and the Ten Commandments would serve as an adequate list of fundamental beliefs. His colleagues refused to accept it, arguing that even a Socinian could sign up to this rather minimal list of beliefs. "I answered them, 'So much the better, and so much the fitter it is to be the matter of our concord.'"[12] His response is likely to have taken their breath away, but he went on to explain that the answer to a new heresy (or even an old one) was not a new formulation of faith. If God had not crafted a statement that no one could misinterpret or give their own sense to, why try to

11 Baxter, *Reliquiae Baxterianae*, 2:204.
12 Baxter, *Reliquiae Baxterianae*, 2:198.

create one? Such a move would only forestall unity, not advance it. "These presumptions and errors have divided and distracted the Christian churches, and one would think experience should save us from them."[13] This was a reasonable point to make but not the best time to make it, with the Socinians prompting such deep anxiety.

More than that, he himself was sounding worryingly Socinian. At this point, Owen was writing his big book against John Biddle, England's most colorful Socinian. Biddle encouraged his readers to be "addicted to none of those many factions in religion, into which the Christian world has to its infinite hurt been divided; but rejoice to be a mere Christian." This was *precisely* the language that Baxter used. Biddle argued that there was no other test of faith than "the Holy Scripture (which all Christians, though otherwise at infinite variance amongst themselves in their opinions about religion, unanimously acknowledge to be the Word of God)."[14] Once again, these were Baxter's exact thoughts. And yet here he was, speaking Socinian sentiments in the context of a subcommittee purposely formed to combat Socinian error!

With the substantive issue raised by Baxter's arrival now recognized and dealt with, the ministers then continued to thrash out the exact details of their formulation. Baxter noted, "When I saw they would not change their method, I saw also that there was nothing for me and others of my mind to do, but only to hinder them from doing harm and thrusting in their own opinions or

---

13 Baxter, *Reliquiae Baxterianae*, 2:198.

14 John Biddle, *A Brief Scripture Catechism for Children: Wherein, Notwithstanding the Brevity Thereof, All Things Necessary unto Life and Godliness Are Contained* (London, 1654), preface, sig. L3r–v.

crude conceits, among our fundamentals." It is easy to imagine Baxter sitting by himself in the back row lobbing objections. It became the clash of personalities that had long been waiting to happen. It seems from his account that most of the group sat in silence while he battled single-handedly with Owen, the "great doer of all that wrote the articles," the man who was "the hotter and better befriended in that assembly." Owen, as we have seen, was not one to be contradicted; all Baxter offered in these meetings was contradiction. He later recalled that "those that managed the business did lack the judgment and accurateness which such work required (though they would think any man supercilious that should tell them so)."[15] No doubt he did tell them so. It is even now astonishing that he could say to Owen's face—the vice-chancellor of Oxford University, the regime's first-choice defender of Christian orthodoxy—that he lacked judgment and accuracy. Baxter, still the new boy on the block, would have seemed patronizing and insulting. No wonder if they accused him of being supercilious, which means "haughtily contemptuous; having or assuming an air of superiority, indifference, or disdain."[16] All that Owen might have suspected from Baxter's written style was confirmed by his personal presence as he set about to make himself an irritant.

The subcommittee succeeded in preparing for the approval of Parliament a definitive list of Christian fundamentals, but their proposal went nowhere, as Parliament was dissolved shortly thereafter. The whole affair achieved nothing except to confirm Baxter

---

15 Baxter, *Reliquiae Baxterianae*, 2:198–99.

16 *Oxford English Dictionary*, s.v. "supercilious," July 2023, https://doi.org/10.1093/OED/1030487195.

and Owen in their worst views of each other and to permanently darken their relationship.

Reflections and Questions

As we look back at these few weeks of mutual frustration for Baxter and Owen, we can see the urgency driving each man's view of the world. Still haunted by the war, Baxter desperately desired an end to all forms of fighting, yet Owen was promoting union by means of a confession that Baxter adamantly believed could only ever serve as an engine of division, and he did this from his platform of vice-chancellor of Oxford University. No wonder it gave Baxter chest pains; he felt there was little ground he could give. For his part, Owen increasingly feared for the future of Trinitarian orthodoxy, and he was right to be worried. What he witnessed was indeed the beginning of a centuries-long partial eclipse. Baxter's theology seemed to hasten the slide with its emphasis on human responsibility in salvation and his adamant determination not to add even one word to the language of Scripture in the effort to shore up the Christian articulation of the deity of the Holy Spirit.

All this mattered. Even so, it is a great shame that the circumstances under which they first met were so inconducive to a mutual understanding. Instead, the work of the subcommittee could only pinpoint their differences and exacerbate the bad temper between them. The great irony is that the project in which Baxter and Owen were involved in 1654 was designed to achieve unity and mend division, but the outcome was the opposite, at least for them. A similar dynamic can play out in our own day, when we or others are so driven by the issues we think are urgent that we override other imperatives that emphasize the priority of unity or, at the least, could help maintain a productive working relationship. And the particular details of how a controversy begins to unfold can all too easily exacerbate those preexisting, unseen, but powerful dimensions of life experience and personality. Once again, these dynamics are well worth pondering.

1. Baxter and Owen allowed their relationship to worsen in the context of a project designed to bring about unity. In other words, working on unity produced division. How do you make sense of that irony? Why did they not pay more attention to unity itself? What could each man have done differently?

2. Think back to a controversy you have witnessed or been a part of. Did the issues that seemed to be at stake merit the discord and division that came about as a result?

3. How much does unity matter? Should we try to set aside genuine and legitimate disagreement to preserve unity? If so, how should we go about it? Are we to preserve unity at all costs? In what circumstances, if any, is disunity a necessary (if regrettable) outcome of holding to the truth as we see it?

4. Once unity has broken down, how can a relationship be repaired? What would it have taken even at this point to bring Owen and Baxter back together?

7

Memory

THE RELATIONSHIP BETWEEN Richard Baxter and John Owen was never going to be easy and amiable. There were too many underlying preconditions to make that possible. Their interactions in print, beginning in 1649, served only to create a mutual distaste that steadily worsened as the 1650s progressed. Matters hardly improved when the two men finally met in 1654; that encounter simply confirmed each man's worst conceptions of the other. By the close of the decade, theirs was a dismal and frayed relationship. And then, just when things could not get any worse, they did. In 1659 their relationship, such as it was, took a fatal turn. In Baxter's eyes, Owen committed his unpardonable sin. Baxter never recovered, and their relationship was never restored. The bitterness between them lingered for the rest of their lives—even beyond their deaths. We are about to see what it was that caused so much hurt and grief.

Rising Confidence and Rapid Collapse

The 1650s was a good decade for Baxter. He looked back on his time at Kidderminster as the best years of his life. The reformation of the parish, so much the fruit of his own intense labor and vision, must have been a profoundly meaningful and satisfying experience for him personally. His fellowship with the other ministers in the Worcestershire Association offered steady encouragement, and his vision was being taken up in other places throughout the nation. We know of twenty-three ministerial associations throughout the counties of England. The movement was not entirely the result of Baxter's pioneering innovation, but it certainly bore his stamp. He now held high hopes of a national reformation, and he would have been justified in feeling that his vision for church unity was working.

Over the decade, he had initiated several attempts at fostering unity between the moderates of all parties. These efforts were largely unsuccessful, but early in 1658 he allowed himself a greater hope. By then he was in negotiations with a fifth group, the Baptists, and the outlook was promising. As he explained in a letter to a friend in November 1658, "I have felt that in my own soul, and seen that upon my brethren for these two or three years past, which persuades me that God is about the healing of our wounds." God had "communicated more healing principles and affections, and poured out more of the Spirit of love and peace than I have perceived heretofore." Perhaps that elusive church unity was now within reach. "The Prince of Peace erects his banner, and the Sons of Peace flock in apace."[1]

1 Richard Baxter to William Allen, November 6, 1658, in Richard Baxter, *Reliquiae Baxterianae, or, Mr. Richard Baxter's Narrative of the Most Memorable Passages of His Life and Times*, ed. Matthew Sylvester (London, 1696), part 3, appendix 4, 81–82.

Furthermore, Baxter was now a figure of national influence, formed on the back of his effectiveness at Kidderminster and his celebrity (and often notoriety) as an author. By the end of 1658, he had published just over thirty books, several of them bestsellers that ran into multiple editions. By 1659, therefore, he was at the top of his game. He had vindicated his ideas in practice. He had come a very long way from the trauma of the English Civil War; he had secured his world. He was at the peak of unprecedented optimism.

An important component in this recent confidence was the death of one Lord Protector, Oliver Cromwell, and the appointment of another, his son Richard Cromwell, in September 1658. Where the father seemed to favor the Congregationalists, his son privileged the Presbyterians. Baxter is typically classed as a Presbyterian, though this label is somewhat misleading. He preferred to be known as a "mere Christian" or "an Episcopal-Presbyterian-Independent."[2] He intended to blend the best of all parties and omit the worst. It was a sensible, moderate approach, but it also reflected that idiosyncratic aspect of his temperament that was never happy except in a party of one. Even so, he could not be more delighted to find a new Lord Protector who favored those whom Baxter favored. The new political realities were pleasing indeed. The future was never brighter.

And then, in a matter of weeks, that future was not so bright. In May 1659 Richard Cromwell was forced to resign as Lord Protector in what was effectively a military coup. The Protectorate had always been propped up by the active support and implicit threat of the army, but by 1659 the lower ranks of officers had lost

---

2   Richard Baxter, *Church History of the Government of Bishops and Their Councils* (London, 1681), sig. b; Baxter, *A Third Defence of the Cause of Peace* (London, 1681), 110.

faith in the house of Cromwell. Under enormous pressure, the army leaders were forced, with genuine reluctance, to betray their promises to Richard Cromwell to support him. By the middle of 1659, he and the Protectorate had been swept away. Long months of chaos came to an end in April 1660 when Parliament invited Charles II to take up the throne of England. The monarchy was restored, as was the Church of England with its elaborate hierarchy of prelates and bishops. Baxter left Kidderminster in April 1660, never to minister there again. His reformation was reversed. The Puritan cause was lost. All the gains of the 1650s were overturned within months. England experienced another "revolution": the turning of the wheel right back to where it started.

Back in April 1659, Baxter was still enjoying the serene isolation of Kidderminster, unaware—yet—of the events taking place in London. He was writing the final chapter of still another book, *A Holy Commonwealth*, in which he laid out his views on the right form of government. Then, on April 25, news arrived from London. It provoked him to write a new final chapter for his book, a collection of "meditations and lamentations" in which he wrestled with his own dismay and disappointment.[3] He berated himself for ever allowing himself to think that he might see anything like heaven on earth. He said that just when we "thought that charity was reviving in the world, new storms arise; our hopes delude us; we find ourselves in the tempestuous ocean, when even now we thought we had been almost at the shore."[4] Just as peace seemed within reach, Baxter's ship had been swept back out into a stormy sea. And he knew whom

---

3   Richard Baxter, *A Holy Commonwealth, or Political Aphorisms, Opening the True Principles of Government* (London, 1659), 491.

4   Baxter, *Holy Commonwealth*, 492.

to blame: the army. When he published *A Holy Commonwealth*, he prefaced it with an angry letter "to all those in the army or elsewhere that have caused our many and great eclipses since 1646."[5]

We cannot know exactly when, but it did not take long for Baxter to find another more particular target for his indignation: John Owen. Owen had fallen from favor with Oliver Cromwell and was no ally of Richard Cromwell, but he continued to be an adviser in national affairs, continued to preach to Parliament, and served as chaplain to the highest-ranking officers in the army. He gathered a congregation at Wallingford House (the London residence of Charles Fleetwood, the army's commander in chief) that comprised most of the army's senior leaders. There, apparently, so Baxter heard second-hand, a meeting was held to discuss the fate of Richard Cromwell. With Owen's active guidance, the army officers decided to take him down. Baxter knew this because a friend of his, Thomas Manton, was just opening the door to enter the room where this discussion was taking place when he heard Owen say, "He must come down, and he shall come down."[6] Apparently, Manton quickly closed the door and walked away. We should appreciate that this evidence is somewhat shaky, relying as it does on a snippet of a sentence heard out of context. The words may or may not have concerned Richard Cromwell; they may or may not have been spoken by Owen. But the damage was done. For our purposes, it is incidental whether Owen's

5   Baxter, *Holy Commonwealth*, preface, sig. A3r.
6   Edmund Calamy, *An Historical Account of My Own Life: With Some Reflections on the Times I Have Lived In (1671–1731)*, ed. John Towhill Rutt, 2 vols. (London: Henry Colburn and Richard Bentley, 1829), 1:378–79; Samuel Parker, ed., *The Noncon-formist's Memorial: Being an Account of the Ministers Who Were Ejected or Silenced after the Restoration* [. . .] *Now Abridged and Corrected by Samuel Parker*, 2 vols. (London: W. Harris, 1775), 1:154.

actions triggered Richard Cromwell's demise or not. What matters is that Baxter found this all too easy to believe. Writing in 1670, he recalled that "Dr. Owen was the greater persuader of Fleetwood, [John] Desborough, and the rest of the officers of the army who were his gathered church, to compel Richard Cromwell to dissolve his parliament; which being done he fell with it."[7]

We know of Owen's alleged machinations because Baxter included them in his autobiography. The *Reliquiae Baxterianae*, eventually published in 1696, five years after he had died, comprises three parts. He wrote the first two parts in 1664 and 1665; the third part took shape in stages as he came back to make additions periodically. We might pause for a moment to consider one paragraph in part 1 in particular. Even in the manuscript, Baxter made several deletions and alterations, so it was a paragraph he worked over quite carefully. It began with these words concerning the downfall of Richard Cromwell: "Dr. Owen and his assistants did the main work." Owen's "confidence and busybodiness and interest in those men did give him the opportunity to do his exploits." He worked the officers around to the conclusion he desired: "Here fasting and prayer, with Dr. Owen's magisterial counsel, did soon determine the case, with the proud and giddy-headed officers, that Richard's Parliament must be dissolved, and then he quickly fell himself."[8] These are several sentences shot through with acute bitterness.

When his editor came along to publish his autobiography, he agonized over what to do with this paragraph. Matthew Sylvester

---

7 Baxter, *Reliquiae Baxterianae*, 3:42.

8 British Library, Egerton MS 2570, fol. 26. This is the manuscript version of Baxter's comments, which is longer, more pointed and more bitter toward Owen. For the abridged, edited version, see Baxter, *Reliquiae Baxterianae*, 1:101.

was a good friend and ministerial colleague of Baxter's, and he wanted to let these words stand exactly as they were written. But his adviser, Edmund Calamy, was horrified. He knew the offense these accusations would cause more than a decade after Owen had died (in 1683). The alleged crime was now over thirty years in the past, and the alleged perpetrator was not alive to defend himself. Calamy later recalled that in the challenging task of wrestling Baxter's massive autobiography into print, their "greatest difficulty" lay with this paragraph. Calamy managed to get Sylvester's agreement to delete or amend some of Baxter's other reflections on Owen, but "with regard to the affair of Wallingford House, and his concern in it, on which Mr. Baxter laid a considerable stress, (and which Mr. Sylvester had often heard Mr. Baxter discourse of with great freedom,) he would not by any means give his consent to take that out."[9] This is in itself an interesting reflection. Sylvester "often" heard Baxter return to Owen's crime, which he talked about "with great freedom." Sylvester knew that he would betray his old friend if he allowed Calamy to have his way. If there was any one thing that Baxter would have been determined to retain in his account of seventeenth-century affairs, this was it. Finally, after long discussion, the two men agreed on a shorter and softer paragraph. Even then, it provoked exactly the degree of outrage that Calamy had feared. Baxter continued to cause offense, then, even from beyond the grave.

Lasting Impact

The relationship between Baxter and Owen had never been a model of warmth and affection; by 1660 it had all but broken

---

9   Calamy, *Historical Account of My Own Life*, 1:377.

down. And that mattered. It had mattered during the 1650s when each one, Owen especially, was a man of influence. But it mattered even more after the monarchy and the bishops of the Church of England were restored in 1660. Many of the older men—and they really were getting old now—scaled back the active leadership that had marked their careers until that point. Thus, a previous generation of leaders gave way, leaving these two men, now in their mid- to late forties, as elder statesmen. Owen became known as the "Atlas of Independency," carrying the Congregationalist cause on his shoulders.[10] One man called Baxter "the Goliath" of the Presbyterians.[11] In the assessment of one eminent historian, Mark Goldie, he was "the figure who towered over Restoration Puritanism."[12] Theirs was the most important relationship within seventeenth-century English Nonconformity. The fault line between Presbyterians and Congregationalists always existed, more apparent at some times than at others, but it would hardly help any sort of reconciliation if their respective leaders did not get along. How could the movement come together when the two leaders' own relationship was marked by so much bitterness and strain?

Furthermore, they continued to pursue rival agendas through-out this post-Restoration period. Baxter favored "comprehension": bringing all godly ministers back within the Church of England

---

10 George Vernon, *A Letter to a Friend concerning Some of Dr. Owen's Principles and Practices* (London, 1670), 36.

11 Thomas Delaune, *Truth Defended, or, A Triple Answer to the Late Triumvirates Opposition on Their Three Pamphlets, viz. Mr. Baxter's Review, Mr. Wills His Censure, Mr Whiston's Postscript to His Essay* (London, 1677), 4.

12 Mark Goldie, gen. ed., *The Entring Book of Roger Morrice, 1677–1691*, vol. 1, *Roger Morrice and the Puritan Whigs* (Woodbridge, UK: Boydell, 2007), 225.

on much more generous terms. Owen wanted toleration: the removal of all legal penalties against those congregations that wished to worship outside the Church of England. These two agendas regularly counteracted each other, allowing those with power to retain it. We might wonder what could have been achieved if those promoting comprehension and toleration had been able to work together. Political realities probably made that impossible, but there could be no real progress without the consent of Owen and Baxter. Achieving a more effective cooperation between those two broad agendas would have required the relationship between these two leading men to be quite different from what it actually was.

There was, though, one attempt to repair the relationship. In late 1669 Baxter heard through the grapevine that Owen had expressed interest in a concord between Congregationalists and Presbyterians. Hearing the news, he "resolved once more to try with Dr. Owen." Even though "all our business with each other had been contradiction"—how true that was—he "thought it [his] duty without any thoughts of former things, to go to him, and be a seeker of peace." According to Baxter, Owen took his visit rather well, though we might observe that Owen was all talk and no action. For his part, Baxter's resolve not to drag up the past inevitably gave way, and his personality took over: "I told him that I must deal freely with him, that when I thought of what he had done formerly I was much afraid lest one that had been so great a breaker would not be made an instrument in healing."[13] He then went on to wonder if Owen's "reputation of former actions" would make it impossible for him now to bring

13 Baxter, *Reliquiae Baxterianae*, 3:61.

his Congregationalists with him into a new era of agreement.[14] So much for not bringing up the past.

Finally, they agreed to draft a set of written proposals that might form the basis of a concord, but Owen made it very clear that he intended to take no part in the drafting. He left that to Baxter. And when Baxter sent his written draft, Owen ignored it for months on end. To hurry him up, Baxter sent him a "chiding" letter.[15] That would seem to be Owen's word for it, and Baxter's letter was typically direct, tactless, heavy-handed, and self-defeating. In the end, Owen returned Baxter's proposal with the briefest of cover notes explaining only that he was "still a well-wisher" to Baxter's attempts at accommodation.[16] There is nothing of warmth here. Though this was a private encounter, each man's personality was on display. It is easy to believe that this fruitless attempt at reconciliation stumbled over Owen's lingering distaste for Baxter and Baxter's inability to forget Owen's past wrongs even when he tried.

There would be no more efforts to seek reconciliation and few interactions between the two men during the 1670s. As time went on, Owen slipped further into old age and ill health. He died at the age of sixty-seven, on August 24, 1683. He was buried at Bunhill Fields in London (where his sepulchre still stands) attended "by near a hundred noblemen's, gentlemen's, and citizens' coaches with six horses each, and a great number of gentlemen in mourning on horseback."[17]

---

14 Baxter, *Reliquiae Baxterianae*, 3:64.

15 Baxter, *Reliquiae Baxterianae*, 3:69.

16 Baxter, *Reliquiae Baxterianae*, 3:69.

17 "The Life of the Late Reverend and Learned John Owen," in *Seventeen Sermons Preached by the Late Reverend and Learned John Owen* (London, 1720), xxxvii. Anthony Wood recorded that there were sixty-seven coaches parked outside at his funeral. Anthony

But Owen's death did not end Baxter's entanglement with him. In the following year, Baxter published a short book critiquing a manuscript reputedly written by Owen.[18] This manuscript argued that it was wrong for Christians to take Communion in parish churches. But that was Baxter's practice, and he leapt into print to defend it. In doing so, he took the reader back to the 1640s and 1650s. He managed to accentuate Owen's near-antinomianism with his comment that Owen "had heard those called Arminians on the one side, and Antinomians on the other, often fluently express their opinions in God's Worship: The former he took to be heinous Errors."[19] Not, as Baxter would have it, the latter: the implicit accusation of antinomianism still hung in the air. And as he traced the damage done by those of a "separating spirit," he came to the consummation of their crimes: "After the death of Oliver, his son was set up, and his Parliament first pulled down (in which the reverend author told me he was an agent) and next himself."[20] The notion that Owen had admitted his part in Richard Cromwell's fall is intriguing but unlikely. Baxter then told the restored bishops that they had Owen to thank for "opening the door, and sweeping the way, and melting down or pulverizing all that was likely to have resisted them." In other words, the blame

---

Wood, *Athenae Oxonienses: An Exact History of all the Writers and Bishops who have had their Education in the* [. . .] *University of Oxford, from* [. . .] *1500 to the Author's Death in November 1695* [. . .], 2nd ed. (London: Knaplock, Midwinter and Tonson, 1721), 2:747.

18 This manuscript is no longer extant, so it is impossible to verify whether Owen was the author or not.

19 Richard Baxter, *An Account of the Reasons Why the Twelve Arguments Said to Be John Owen's Change Not My Judgment about Communion with Parish Churches*, book 3 in *Catholick Communion Defended against Both Extreams* (London, 1684), 21.

20 Baxter, *Account of the Reasons*, 27.

for the current predicament of Nonconformists rested with Owen's actions in 1659. Baxter clarified, "I speak not of the intentions, but of the action."[21] Even so, that is quite some accusation.

The timing and content of the book do Baxter little credit, but he saved his most graceless moment until the end. He imagined Owen in heaven repenting over his position against parish Communion. To underline the point, he wrote a long paragraph that put words in Owen's mouth: "I was of too narrow mistaken principles, and in the time of temptation I did not foresee to what Church-confusion, and dissolution, and hatred, and ruin, dividing practices of some did tend."[22] Baxter's arrogance in presuming to speak not just for someone who was dead but for someone whom he had attacked, opposed, and misinterpreted for most of his career is really quite stunning. "No doubt but now this is Dr. Owen's mind."[23] Baxter was so utterly convinced that he was right, and Owen wrong, that he would dare to constrain Owen's heavenly joy and peace. When others criticized him for his tactlessness and insensitivity, he simply reasserted his position. Yet when they accused him of unforgiveness against Owen, he did say this: "If I know my heart, I forgave, and fully let go all personal quarrel long ago: but the national concerns made so deep a wound in my heart, as never will be fully healed in this world."[24] It is doubtful that Baxter had forgiven Owen quite as well as he thought he had, but he spoke the truth and spoke his heart when he opened

21 Baxter, *Account of the Reasons*, 29.

22 Baxter, *Account of the Reasons*, postscript, sig. M4.

23 Baxter, *Account of the Reasons*, postscript, sig. M4v.

24 Richard Baxter, *Catholick Communion Doubly Defended: By Dr. Owens Vindicator, and Richard Baxter. And the State of That Communion Opened* (London, 1684), 7.

up about his wounds. The disaster of 1659 and the dashing of all his hopes and dreams made such a deep wound that he really did never recover while in this world.

In time, his turn came to leave it. Baxter died several hours before dawn on December 8, 1691, at the age of seventy-six. Edward Harley, one of the executors of his will, remarked that London had never "seen such vast numbers of people to attend any funeral. The streets and windows and balconies were all crowded, from Merchant Taylors Hall to Christ Church [Newgate] where he was interred [beside the grave of] his wife."[25] Regrettably, the church was damaged by the war in 1941 and subsequently demolished, removing any physical testimony to their life and death. But Baxter left enough other evidence to mark his passing, not least in bequeathing the manuscript of his autobiography to his young friend Matthew Sylvester. It contained within it one last glancing blow against Owen. That paragraph of the "Wallingford House affair" was like an incendiary device that Baxter buried under the ground for three decades, ready to explode after his death. The bitterness between the two men did not end even with the grave.

Reflections and Questions

Our view of reality is only ever partial. We see the world through a filter shaped by experience and colored by memory. We assess the actions of others through that filter, which can too easily distort our perceptions. So it was with Baxter and Owen. We simply do not know the extent to which Owen was complicit in the downfall of Richard Cromwell. He certainly moved in the relevant circles,

25 [Richard Ward, ed.], *The Manuscripts of His Grace the Duke of Portland Preserved at Welbeck Abbey* (London: Her Majesty's Stationery Office, 1894), 3:485.

but it is hard to believe that he was the sole or even the most influential engineer of events. The fact is that 1659 was a disastrous year for him as well. His worry that a coup was imminent made him literally ill. If Baxter had ever chosen to ask, he might have been surprised by the extent to which Owen shared his disappointment and the sense that his dreams had been crushed. But for Baxter, it was entirely plausible that Owen was the critical agent in bringing down the Protectorate—and all his cherished hopes and dreams along with it. Baxter's previous experience and recollections deeply prejudiced him to believe the very worst of Owen. It seems likely that Thomas Manton's recollection of Owen's words ("He must come down") immediately rang true to Baxter. Ever after, he could not bring himself to forget or, despite the best of intentions, forgive. He now looked at Owen through a prism of past hurts and offense. All Owen's actions—from his first written reply in 1650 to his neglect of Baxter's papers in the late 1660s—steadily formed a picture in Baxter's mind that was entirely unappealing but not entirely fair. He was simply too ready to believe the worst. The events of 1659 now served as a distorting lens through which he discerned all previous events.

We might call this "fatal memory": whether we realize it or not, we allow the past to shape our perceptions of the present in ways that are inaccurate and unhelpful. This raises many deep issues of trust and forgiveness, but having observed the lingering aftertaste of 1659 in the subsequent relationship of these two men, we might reflect on the implications for our own day. Human nature has not changed, and the dynamics we have witnessed are not unfamiliar. This raises a number of questions that are worth our reflection.

1. Why is it that we tend to see the actions of others in the worst possible light and our own actions in the best possible light? How might we attain a more objective and balanced perspective?

2. What do you make of Baxter's claim that he had forgiven Owen? Can we say that we have forgiven someone and then hold on to the memory of their offense with such tenacity as Baxter demonstrated? What does forgiveness entail? How can we help our wounds heal?

3. Once a series of hurts and grievances has accumulated, how can we set them aside or at least prevent them from dominating and distorting our view of the other person? Think back to 1659 and 1660: What could Baxter and Owen have done differently to improve their view of each other?

4. From what you have just read, what was the impact of the broken relationship between these two important leaders? Why did it matter? What was the impact of a controversy you have witnessed or been a part of? How can we try to limit the damage when discord breaks out?

5. In the conclusion that follows, we ask ourselves what might have been done differently to prevent the breakdown in the relationship between Owen and Baxter. Now that you have followed the whole story, how would you answer that question? What might have helped prevent this outcome of mutual alienation and distrust?

Conclusion

JOHN OWEN AND RICHARD BAXTER were giants of seventeenth-century English Christianity. Their achievements, not least their literary achievements, were nothing short of astonishing—and profoundly important. Both men demonstrated impressive godliness and humility. Owen rarely spoke about himself in his writings, believing that the world would have little interest in him personally. Baxter, we might recall, spoke of himself merely as "a pen in God's hand, and what praise is due to a pen?"[1] They were both wise, insightful, passionate, warmly committed to Jesus Christ, and deeply concerned for his church and the gospel. Their lives embodied steadfast effort and impressive fruit that endures to the present day. Yet for all their evident strengths, they had their flaws. For all the qualities they held in common, they fell out with each other. Their story is a mix of greatness and fallibility. How are we to make sense of it, and what can we learn from it?

The reality is that even the most conscientious Christians disagree. It is their very conscientiousness that can trigger their

---

1 William Bates, *A Funeral Sermon for Richard Baxter*, 2nd ed. (London, 1692), 125.

disagreement. They take truth seriously. It matters. It matters enough to take a stand, even against a fellow believer. As Baxter said, "Their very heart is set upon these heavenly things, and therefore they cannot make light of the smallest truth of God, and this may be some occasion of their difference." In contrast, "the ungodly differ not about religion because they have no religion to differ about." So Baxter would rather have the "discord of the saints" than the "concord of the wicked."[2] He makes a fair point. Contentious issues inflame passion out of deep and genuine conviction, and we cannot set such conviction lightly aside. I want to respect Baxter and Owen's differences, not just regret them.

Still, Baxter's reflections serve rather too well to justify the inclination in his personality to defend "even the smallest truth" regardless of the cost to personal relationships. It is all too easy for us to do the same and to rationalize our motives for engaging in conflict. Not all disagreement stems from a high-minded concern for the truth. To quote Baxter further, "It is the interest of Satan to divide the servants of Christ," and the enemies of the church love nothing more than to stir up dissension "that they may fish in troubled waters."[3] We may tell ourselves that our motivations are noble and our cause is just, but as the story of Owen and Baxter has demonstrated, such justifications are suspect, and the damage caused by conflict can last a lifetime.

I have thought a lot about this story over recent years, and I keep asking myself what might have been different. Is there anything that could have changed the outcome or prevented the

---

2 Richard Baxter, *Catholic Unity, or The Only Way to Bring Us All to Be of One Religion* (London, 1660), 293.

3 Baxter, *Catholic Unity*, 296, 298.

worst of their conflict? If we can identify what could have helped them, we might at the same time gain insight into what can help us in our own disagreements or help those around us who are caught up in conflict. Let me offer five possibilities.

To begin with, it is a shame that there was no one to mediate between them. Earlier in the seventeenth century, similar disagreements had strained Puritan relationships, but those divisions were kept hidden from public view for the most part and moderated by well-oiled mechanisms designed to bring about at least a productive working relationship. Differences were negotiated. A respected senior leader could be called on to intervene. A "disputation" might be held (a semipublic debate) in which the disputants had the opportunity to present their case. But by the 1640s those mechanisms had broken down. Until then, all books had to receive a license before they could be published, but with the collapse of censorship, anyone could put their thoughts in print. Baxter did, and Owen replied. There was little that could be done to repair those first impressions made in the open view of all. The very public nature of Baxter's comments partly explains Owen's compulsion to respond, also in public and also in print. There was no one to bring them together and no practical way of doing it. With Baxter in Kidderminster and Owen in Ireland, the geographical distance between them was too great to bridge. So a dispute that was at least in some measure more about personality than about theology was left to fester. When the two men did finally meet, it seems that no one in that 1654 subcommittee had the stature and wisdom to guide them to a meeting of minds. Perhaps the participants lacked the will. Those general differences between Congregationalists and Presbyterians would have provided little incentive (and every disincentive) toward a mutual understanding between these two leading players. There is no evidence that anyone observed their mutual antipathy and sought to mediate a reconciliation. It looks as though Christian community failed to moderate the worst impulses in each of these men because that community was itself divided.

Second, it would have helped if Owen and Baxter had been able to focus more on what held them together and less on what drove them apart. They agreed on a great deal; they even admitted as much. The differences between them were relatively narrow. If only they could have recognized how much they shared in common and focused on that. Instead, they could see only their differences. This illustrates a general pattern: those who are closest to each other have the bitterest disagreements—the smallest differences assume an overlarge importance, while outsiders look on and wonder what all the fuss is about. It was difficult for these two men to recognize their commonalities when contingent circumstances pinpointed their differences with excruciating precision. Their personalities intervened, and they were big personalities. We might call them alpha males. Self-awareness might have softened each man's blows against the other. Both were at fault, both were fallible, and yet both struggled to see it or admit it. The problem always lay in the other man.

Third, in addition to focusing on their common ground, they might also have paid far more attention to those many verses in Scripture that summon us to unity and concord. This is, after all, a driving theme through the whole of the Bible. "Behold, how good and pleasant it is / when brothers dwell in unity!" (Ps. 133:1). On the night before he died, Jesus prayed to the Father for all his disciples, "Keep them in your name . . . that they may be one, even as we are one" (John 17:11). That is a high prayer indeed. We see the same concern expressed throughout the letters of Paul. He instructed the Philippian Christians, "Complete my joy by being of the same mind, having the same love, being in full accord and of one mind" (Phil. 2:2). He called on the believers at Thessalonica, "Be at peace among yourselves" (1 Thess. 5:13). He gave a similar command to the church in Rome: "If possible, so far as it depends on you, live peaceably with all" (Rom. 12:18). Scripture seems clear on this point: disunity, discord, and division are a reproach to the cause of Christ. Yet it seems that such verses were obscured in Baxter's and Owen's mind because the differences between them loomed so large. Theirs was a contentious age in which printed disputations were hardly uncommon, but even so, they did not seem to pause to ask themselves whether the issues at stake really justified setting aside these repeated biblical injunctions toward unity. Both men genuinely believed in unity, yet they seemed blind to the way that their own actions cut across that very goal.

Fourth, the story of Baxter and Owen has reinforced for me the importance of one central virtue: humility. As I look back over the events of this book, I see far too much pride in both men. Oddly enough, they had no trouble seeing that pride in the other man, but each one struggled to see it in himself. Paul urged the believers in Ephesus, "Walk in a manner worthy of the calling to which you have been called, with all humility and gentleness, with patience, bearing with one another in love, eager to maintain the unity of the Spirit in the bond of peace" (Eph. 4:1–3). The story we have just encountered would have been transformed if these two Christian brothers had carried themselves in that manner.

I was once told that there is no problem in the world that cannot be solved by humility—humility from all those involved. If Owen and Baxter had responded to each other with generosity, with an understanding of their own fallibility and weakness, and with the "humility and gentleness" that Paul so prized, their relationship might have been a great deal better than it was, and their story could have been different. If they could have thought the best of each other, not the worst, they might not have wounded each other in the way that they did. This is a story of pride, willfulness, and self-blindness when it could, potentially, have been a story of forgiveness, understanding, and generosity even in the face of legitimate difference.

Finally, it would have helped if they could see what we can see. This is the great advantage of distance and hindsight, an advantage that is by definition unavailable to the participants in any controversy. We have noticed how accidental factors triggered what may have been an unnecessary controversy. We have identified the ways in which this was more a clash of personalities than it was a clash of ideas. We have been able to examine in slow motion the breakdown of their relationship. Over time, and left unresolved, wounds began to accumulate, piled so high it was impossible to see past them. This was a long process of alienation in which action gave way to emotion early on. The issue no longer resided merely in intellectual differences on certain points of belief but in the strong feelings that were provoked by such differences. Those feelings were not an inevitable consequence; it is entirely possible for two people to disagree amicably. But this is far more difficult in a context like theirs in which trust has been lost. In its place, instincts of fear and opposition are aroused, and all future actions are assessed through that filter of mistrust. Memory—often a partial, prejudiced, and inaccurate memory—proves to be a powerful shaping influence long after the initial events have occurred. This is memory as an open wound. As Baxter so eloquently explained, "The national concerns made so deep a wound in my heart, as never will be fully healed in this world."[4] I would think the same was true of Owen. He might also have harbored the memory of Baxter's irritations along the way, not least his obstinacy in 1654.

We have been able to see the various causes of their conflict and the different factors at work as their relationship went from bad to worse, but they could not see them. They were far too close and far too personally invested. It is the same with us. If we are engaged in controversy, we become blind to so much of what is going on, not least inside us. That, I hope, has been the value of this book. In understanding their story, perhaps we can better understand our own narratives. If we can see what they missed, perhaps we will have a much clearer idea of what we may be missing. Owen and Baxter have inadvertently supplied us with a checklist of questions that we might use as we adapt our response to discord when it begins and as it proceeds:

- Do I *really* need to respond to the initial provocation?
- How much of the conflict can be traced back to personality rather than theology?
- Am I overlooking all the things I have in common with the other person and seeing only the small number of differences?

4 Richard Baxter, *Catholick Communion Doubly Defended: By Dr. Owens Vindicator, and Richard Baxter. And the State of That Communion Opened* (London, 1684), 7.

- How are my own faults contributing to a poor relationship?
- Am I showing the humility, generosity, gentleness, and kindness to which I am called?
- How much pride is mixed up in my motivations and actions?
- How much damage will be inflicted on those around me and the cause of Christ by my continued conflict with the other person?
- Is there anyone in my Christian community who can help repair our relationship or manage our differences?

If we approach these questions with openness and self-awareness, we may be better able to manage our part in any conflict. Thus the story of Owen and Baxter is an extremely useful and illuminating one. It has left us with a lot to think about.

1. Having explored the strained relationship between Owen and Baxter, how would you explain the discord between them? How does your account of their difficulties help you understand your own?

2. In your own controversies or those around you, what mechanisms are there for mediation? How does it help to bring in a mediator, especially when strong personalities are involved? What are the risks when there is no one to intervene?

3. Why is it that Christians too easily set aside the many commands in Scripture toward unity and the "humility and

gentleness" that requires? Similarly, why do we fail to see the vast common ground we share and focus only on our narrow differences? How can we maintain a clear vision of our unity and affinity when conflict first breaks out?

4. Can you explain how two great leaders of the past, two good men, could possess such profound flaws and weaknesses? What does that say about human weakness and sinfulness? Should we accept similar weaknesses in others, or should we challenge them?

5. This has been a story with no happy ending. Should we accept that some relationships break down? At what point, if at all, should we stop working toward reconciliation and accept that while we live in this world, not every Christian brother or sister is going to get along?

6. "If possible, so far as it depends on you, live peaceably with all." These words in Romans 12:18 indicate that it's not always possible to live in peace with another person. What is our responsibility in such a situation?

7. At the end of this story, what is one thing that, above all, you will take with you in your future relationships?

.

Chronology

THIS CHRONOLOGY is not intended to be an exhaustive time line. It instead offers a selection of events that broadly reflect the content of the book.

Date	National Events	Richard Baxter	John Owen
November 12, 1615	—	Richard Baxter is born	—
1616	—	—	John Owen is born
1625	Charles I becomes king of England and marries Princess Henrietta Maria of France	—	—
1628	—	—	Owen enters Oxford University
1629	Charles I begins his eleven-year "personal rule" without summoning Parliament	—	—

Date	National Events	Richard Baxter	John Owen
1630	William Laud becomes archbishop of Canterbury	—	—
1632	—	—	Owen graduates with a bachelor of arts
December 1632	—	—	Owen is ordained a deacon
1633 or 1634	—	Baxter teaches at Wroxeter School for three months	—
1635	—	—	Owen graduates with a master of arts
1637	Charles I introduces a new prayer book in Scotland	—	Owen leaves Oxford University to become a private tutor
February 29, 1638	Scottish ministers sign a national covenant that unites Scottish resistance to the religious innovations of Charles I and William Laud	—	—
December 1638	—	—	Owen is ordained a priest

Date	National Events	Richard Baxter	John Owen
December 18, 1638	—	Baxter is appointed first master of Dudley Grammar School and is licensed to teach	—
December 23, 1638	—	Baxter is ordained a deacon	—
March–June 1639	The First Bishops' War (i.e., the invasion of England by Scottish forces)	—	—
autumn 1639	—	Baxter moves to Bridgnorth as assistant to the vicar William Madstard	—
April–May 1640	The Short Parliament sits	—	—
August–October 1640	The Second Bishops' War	—	—
November 3, 1640	The Long Parliament begins to sit	—	—
April 5, 1641	—	Baxter is chosen as lecturer at Kidderminster effectively to replace the inadequate ministry of the vicar George Dance	—

Date	National Events	Richard Baxter	John Owen
September 28, 1641	The House of Commons orders the removal of all Laudian innovations in churches	—	—
October 23, 1641	A Catholic rebellion breaks out in Ireland	—	—
1642	—	—	Owen moves to London and experiences a moment of conversion and assurance
July 9, 1642	Parliament votes to raise an army	—	—
late summer 1642	—	In the face of Royalist hostility, Baxter withdraws from Kidderminster to Gloucester for one month	—
September 23, 1642	—	Baxter witnesses the ambush at Powick Bridge	—
October 23, 1642	The first battle of the English Civil War at Edgehill	Baxter preaches at Alcester, where he can hear the cannon fire in the nearby battle	—
October 24, 1642	—	Baxter visits the battlefield at Edgehill	—

Date	National Events	Richard Baxter	John Owen
late October 1642	—	Baxter leaves Kidderminster for Coventry, where he spends over two years preaching to the garrison	—
1643	—	—	Owen publishes his first book, *A Display of Arminianism*, and becomes minister of Fordham in Essex
July 1, 1643	The first meeting of the Westminster Assembly	—	—
late 1643	—	—	Owen marries Mary Rooke
January 4, 1645	The Book of Common Prayer is abolished, and a new Directory for Public Worship takes its place	—	—
January 10, 1645	Archbishop William Laud is executed	—	—
February 15, 1645	Parliament's military forces are reconfigured according to a "New Model"	—	—

Date	National Events	Richard Baxter	John Owen
June 15, 1645	The battle of Naseby turns the course of the war	—	—
June 16, 1645	—	Baxter visits Naseby the day after the battle and as a consequence enlists as an army chaplain	—
April 1646	—	—	Owen becomes the minister of Coggeshall in Essex and preaches to Parliament a sermon that is published as *A Vision of Unchangeable Free Mercy*
May 5, 1646	Charles I surrenders to the Scottish army at Southwell	—	—
February 1647	—	Baxter is taken seriously ill, and as he recuperates over the next few months, he begins to write *The Saints' Everlasting Rest*	—

Date	National Events	Richard Baxter	John Owen
May 1647	—	Baxter returns to his pastoral ministry in Kidderminster	—
February 1648	—	—	Owen publishes *The Death of Death in the Death of Christ*
July 1648	Scottish forces enter England and are defeated by Oliver Cromwell at the battle of Preston	—	—
August 1648	Royalist forces lay siege to Colchester	—	Owen serves as army chaplain during the siege of Colchester
January 30, 1649	After a trial by the High Court of Justice, Charles I is executed	—	—
January 31, 1649	—	—	Owen preaches a sermon to Parliament the day after the regicide that is published as *The Shaking and Translating of Heaven and Earth*
early 1649	—	Baxter publishes his first book, *Aphorisms of Justification*	—

Date	National Events	Richard Baxter	John Owen
February–March 1649	The monarchy and the House of Lords are abolished	—	—
April 20, 1649	—	—	Owen meets Cromwell for the first time
August–October 1649	Cromwell suppresses the Irish rebellion, returning to England on May 28, 1650	—	Owen serves as a chaplain to Cromwell while in Ireland
February 1650	—	Baxter publishes his second book, *The Saints' Everlasting Rest*	—
July–December 1650	Cromwell invades Scotland to prevent Charles II from retaking the crown	—	Owen serves as a chaplain to Cromwell while in Scotland
September 1650	—	—	Owen responds to Baxter in *Of the Death of Christ*
March 18, 1651	—	—	Owen is appointed dean of Christ Church, Oxford University
July 1651	Charles II invades England but is defeated in September by Cromwell's forces	—	Owen ceases to act as a chaplain to Cromwell but continues as a chaplain to the Council of State

Date	National Events	Richard Baxter	John Owen
mid-1652	—	Baxter begins to create the Worcestershire Association of neighboring ministers	—
September 26, 1652	—	—	Owen is appointed vice-chancellor of Oxford University and created a doctor of divinity
mid-1653	—	Baxter publishes *Christian Concord*, which sets out the common pastoral practice of the ministers in the Worcestershire Association	—
December 1653	The Protectorate is created, and Cromwell is installed as Lord Protector	—	—
November 4–December 12, 1654	A subcommittee meets to advise Parliament on the fundamentals of the faith	Baxter takes part in the subcommittee	Owen takes part in the subcommittee
December 24, 1654	—	Baxter preaches to Parliament a sermon published as *Humble Advice*	—

Date	National Events	Richard Baxter	John Owen
January 1655	—	Baxter publishes his *Confession of His Faith*, which includes a response to Owen	—
April 1655	—	—	Owen publishes a massive work against the Socinians called *Vindiciae Evangelicae, or, The Mystery of the Gospel Vindicated* and responds to Baxter's *Confession* in a brief work appended to the end called *Of the Death of Christ and of Justification*
early 1656	—	Baxter publishes *The Agreement of Diverse Ministers of Christ in the County of Worcester for Catechizing or Personal Instructing* that sets out the ministers' agreed-on practice of family visitation	—

Date	National Events	Richard Baxter	John Owen
July 1656	—	Baxter publishes *The Reformed Pastor*	—
March–May 1657	Cromwell is offered but eventually declines the title of king	—	Owen opposes Cromwell's inclination to take the title of king
June 1657	—	—	Owen publishes *Of Schism*
October 9, 1657	—	—	Owen is replaced as vice-chancellor of Oxford University
September 3, 1658	Oliver Cromwell dies	—	—
September 4, 1658	Richard Cromwell is declared Lord Protector	—	—
March 1659	—	—	Owen gathers a church at Wallingford House, the London residence of Charles Fleetwood, the army's commander in chief
April 23, 1659	Members of Parliament are locked out of Parliament by the army	—	—

Date	National Events	Richard Baxter	John Owen
April 25, 1659	—	Baxter breaks off writing *A Holy Commonwealth* to pen a series of "lamentations and meditations" provoked by the army's coup	—
May 25, 1659	Richard Cromwell resigns as Lord Protector	—	—
July 1659	—	Baxter publishes *A Holy Commonwealth*	—
March 13, 1660	—	—	Owen is removed as dean of Christ Church, Oxford University
April 13, 1660	—	Baxter arrives in London to play a part in finding a religious settlement for England	—
May 1, 1660	Parliament votes to restore the monarchy	—	—
May 25, 1660	Charles II returns to London	—	—
June 13, 1660	The bishops are restored to the House of Lords	—	—

Date	National Events	Richard Baxter	John Owen
mid-1660	—	Baxter engages in a series of meetings regarding a religious settlement	—
July 1661	—	Baxter is a leading figure in the Savoy Conference, an unsuccessful attempt to find compromise with the restored bishops	—
May 25, 1662	—	Baxter makes it known that he will not conform to the requirements of the Act of Uniformity, thus ending his public ministry	—
July 19, 1662	The Act of Uniformity becomes law	—	—
August 24, 1662	The provisions of the Act of Uniformity come into force	—	—
September 10, 1662	—	Baxter marries Margaret Charlton	—

Date	National Events	Richard Baxter	John Owen
1664–1665	—	Baxter writes the first and second part of his autobiography, in which he bitterly criticizes Owen for his actions	—
1669–1670	—	Baxter approaches Owen in a fruitless attempt at reconciliation	—
January 28, 1677	—	—	Owen's wife, Mary, dies
June 1678	—	—	Owen marries Dorothy D'Oyley
August 24, 1683	—	—	Owen dies
1684	—	Baxter criticizes Owen in *An Account of the Reasons Why the Twelve Arguments Said to Be John Owen's Change Not My Judgment about Communion with Parish Churches*	—
December 8, 1691	—	Baxter dies	—
May or June 1696	—	Baxter's autobiography, *Reliquiae Baxterianae*, is published	—

Glossary

THIS GLOSSARY of key terms is designed to help you understand the story of Richard Baxter and John Owen that unfolds in this book.

antinomians/antinomianism. Antinomianism was a style of doctrine that placed all the initiative and action in salvation with God and none with the believer. Taking their cue from Martin Luther (see **Reformation**), the antinomians believed salvation was literally and without qualification by faith alone, without works, and entirely from God's "free grace." The label *antinomian* means "against the law," which carried the implication that antinomians did not hold to the moral law (or any law) and would live as they pleased, believing that God did not see any sin in his children. Baxter feared that antinomianism would result in loose living, and he all but accused Owen of being an antinomian. The antinomians were reacting against what they saw as a dangerous moralism within Puritanism, in which believers were expected to engage in an arduous battle against sin in all its forms. Antinomians argued that this was merely "works righteousness" dressed up in the language of the Reformation.

archbishop of Canterbury. The Church of England comprised two provinces, one in the south, centered in Canterbury, and the other in the north, centered in York, but it was the archbishop of Canterbury who held the acknowledged primacy among all bishops and archbishops. While the monarch was the Supreme Head of the Church of England, the archbishop of Canterbury exercised significant leadership in the governance and practice of the national church and thus carried enormous influence over the country as a whole.

Arminianism. A style of doctrine that emphasizes human choice and free will in salvation rather than God's election and predestination of the elect. It takes its name from a Dutch theologian, Jacobus Arminius. While it was officially repudiated at the Synod of Dort (1618–1619), in which the British delegates played a leading role, Arminianism subsequently grew in popularity and influence, eventually eclipsing Calvinism as its main rival in England. Baxter was accused of being an Arminian, though he consistently denied the accusation.

Baptists. The seventeenth century is too early to talk of denominations in England. The Baptists were very much a minority grouping among the Puritans. They were Congregationalists who distinguished themselves by practicing adult baptism and repudiating infant baptism, believing it had no precedent in the Scriptures. Both Owen and Baxter supported infant baptism, but both were prepared to work with Baptists in the cause of unity.

Calvinism. A style of doctrine that emphasizes God's election and predestination of the elect in salvation rather than human choice and free will. It takes its name from John Calvin, a

French theologian who came to fame at Geneva and was closely identified with the Reformation as it took shape in the Swiss territories (see **Reformed theology**). Owen consistently defended Calvinism through the whole course of his life, though his efforts failed to halt the tide that swept Calvinism from its place of prominence during his lifetime.

catechism. A learning tool for both children and adults. A catechism was structured in the form of questions and answers that articulated the central beliefs of the Christian faith. Those being "catechized" would memorize all the answers so that they could respond accurately when tested. Both Baxter and Owen employed a catechism in their pastoral ministry.

church discipline. The process of dealing with visible sin within a church community based on the teaching of Jesus in Matthew 18:15–17. In essence, sin was to be confronted first in private and then, if necessary, in public. If the sinner refused to repent, he or she would be excommunicated or banished from the church community. In any English parish (especially at a time when the law required every person to attend church, from the most godly to the least), implementing a form of church discipline was difficult and fraught, but both Baxter and Owen urged its use.

Communion. The sacrament of bread and wine taken in what is also called the Lord's Supper.

comprehension. In the wake of the Restoration and with the subsequent development of Nonconformity, many of those shut out of church ministry sought a way back in. They wanted the terms of belonging to be widened in order to "comprehend" moderate Puritans who would not otherwise have chosen to leave the church in the first place. The agenda for comprehension competed with the rival agenda for toleration, which sought legal recognition of Christian groups outside the Church of England. Baxter and the Presbyterians favored comprehension; Owen and the Congregationalists favored toleration.

confession. A statement of faith that marked out the specific beliefs of a particular group. During the sixteenth century, such confessions proliferated as separate Protestant groups emerged in the wake of the Reformation, so this is often looked on as an era of "confessionalization." Baxter inherently distrusted confessions because of their capacity to perpetuate conflict and division rather than end them, but Owen saw confessions as an essential means toward unity. See also **creed.**

Congregationalists/Congregationalism. Congregationalists believed that each local congregation possessed full church authority in itself, with power distributed between the elders and the congregation. This included the power to call a new minister or excommunicate a member (see **church discipline**). No other external authority existed: not bishops, not a synod (a meeting of regional or national leaders). Congregationalists disliked the mixed nature of the parish system, in which the godly worshiped alongside the ungodly, so they formed distinct congregations with voluntary membership of the "visible saints." Owen was a leading Congregationalist figure. Baxter was sympathetic to their vision of the local congregation but intensely disliked separatism, which he saw as a logical outcome of Congregationalist practice and as undermining the evangelistic power inherent in England's parish church structure.

creed. A simple statement of essential Christian beliefs designed to be easily memorized. Among the best-known examples are the Apostles' Creed and the Nicene Creed. Baxter believed that these (along with the Lord's Prayer) were a sufficient basis for unity among Christians.

crown. The sovereignty, authority, or dominion of which a royal crown is the symbol. This is another word for the rule, position, or government of a monarch.

discipline. See **church discipline**.

Dissenters. See **Nonconformists/Nonconformity**.

doctrine. Another word for Christian belief or theology. Doctrine was often a matter of dispute among seventeenth-century English Christians and Christian groups.

elect/election. The elect were those whom God predestined or elected to salvation before the creation of the world. Calvinists understood election solely as the choice of a sovereign God to elect some individuals for salvation (and not others) so that their perseverance and ultimate salvation could never be in doubt. Arminians saw the elect as a group of "those who have faith," so it was for any individual to choose whether he or she would join that group by having faith. See also **predestination**.

English Civil War. The English Civil War was, in fact, a series of three episodes of conflict. It is also known as the "War of Three Kingdoms" because the wars involved the three nations of England, Scotland, and Ireland. The First Civil War took place from 1642 to 1646 and ended with the surrender of King Charles I. The Second Civil War was over in a matter of months in 1648 and resulted in Charles's execution in January 1649 (see **regicide**). The Third Civil War (1649–1651) involved conflict in Scotland (preventing the return of King Charles II) and in Ireland (finally suppressing the Irish Rebellion of 1641).

Episcopalian. This view of church governance places a high priority on diocesan bishops. A diocese is a large geographical area comprising hundreds of parishes overseen by a bishop who carried ultimate responsibility for the many thousands of souls under his spiritual jurisdiction. Both Baxter and Owen felt that this was unscriptural and unworkable. For them, such oversight was best concentrated in the individual parish or congregation, where the minister (we could call him an "overseer" or "bishop" following some translations of 1 Tim. 3:1) knew each person by name.

Erastians. The Erastians take their name from Thomas Lieber, known as Erastus, a sixteenth-century Swiss theologian who believed that if a nation had a godly ruler, there was no need for any other authority in the church. In England, that conviction took the form of suspicion of England's ministers and a resolve always to keep the church under the authority of Parliament. The Erastians particularly distrusted a Presbyterian or Congregationalist model of church governance, which located church authority within a presbytery (a body of local elders from different parishes) or within the confines of a single congregation, respectively.

fundamentals. In the wake of the English Civil War, heresy appeared to be flourishing in England, to the alarm of many. A line needed to be drawn on what ideas and practices could fall under toleration and which were unsupportable. The fundamentals of the faith were those Christian beliefs that were considered essential for salvation. Anyone who adhered to the fundamentals would be tolerated. But it proved impossible for an agreed list of fundamental beliefs to be approved by Parliament, despite Owen's best efforts. Baxter was pleased when the effort came to nothing, and he was doubtful such an approach would bring about unity. See also **confession** and **Scripture sufficiency.**

heretics/heresy. Heresy is the label attached to versions of Christian belief that lay outside the bounds of orthodoxy. These beliefs were not simply open to debate or differing interpretation; they were dangerous and utterly wrong, undermining the very fabric of the Christian faith. Often such ideas had been declared to be heresy by a previous church council, but heresy was also an easy label to throw around in order to discredit an opponent.

Interregnum. An interregnum is a period "between the reigns" of one monarch and another. In seventeenth-century England, the Interregnum is the period from January 1649 (when King Charles I was executed [see **regicide**]) to May 1660 (the Restoration of King Charles II). During this period, England was a republic. In the time of the Protectorate, governing power was shared between Parliament and the Lord Protector.

Jesuits. The name given to members of the Society of Jesus, a Roman Catholic order formed by Ignatius of Loyola in 1540 that sent undercover missionaries into England to support Catholics there. It was assumed, particularly by Baxter, that they were part of clandestine efforts to retake the country for Catholicism. In their doctrine of salvation, the Jesuits generally emphasized human free will and responsibility.

Nonconformists/Nonconformity. In the wake of the Restoration of the monarchy in 1660, the 1662 Act of Uniformity required all church ministers to give their full assent to everything written in the Book of Common Prayer and to renounce a vow taken by most Puritans during the mid-1640s called the Solemn League and Covenant. Around two thousand Puritan ministers could not in good conscience conform to these requirements, and they were ejected from their place of ministry in the Church of England. So from 1662 we talk about Nonconformists or Dissenters rather than Puritans, though the individuals and their distinctive concerns did not change very much. Baxter and Owen were the two most important leaders within Nonconformity.

orthodox/orthodoxy. Orthodoxy represents correct Christian belief, theology, or doctrine (as opposed to heresy). Often these beliefs had been sanctioned by an earlier church council and encapsulated in a creed.

parish. The parish was the basic geographical and administrative district of the Church of England, which comprised around nine thousand parishes. Each parish comprised only one church with at least one minister; everyone living in that parish—from the genuinely devout to the uninterested—was expected to attend that church. Congregationalism threatened to unsettle the integrity of a parish by allowing the possibility of a distinct congregation within the confines of the parish, a congregation made up of only the devout. Baxter's parish of Kidderminster comprised between three and four thousand people; some parishes, especially those in the cities, could be even larger.

Parliament. England's traditional constitution was formed around the executive power of the king to govern and the power of the two houses of Parliament—the House of Commons and the House of Lords—to approve taxation and propose legislation. The House of Commons represented those with land or money; the House of Lords comprised the aristocracy and the bishops of the Church of England. After the regicide in 1649, England abolished both the monarchy and the House of Lords, thus leaving executive government in the hands of the House of Commons until the development of the Protectorate in December 1653. At the Restoration in 1660, both the monarchy and the House of Lords were reestablished.

predestination. Built on Ephesians 1:4–6 and 11–12 and other biblical texts, predestination refers to the idea that God has predestined to salvation certain individuals known as the elect, choosing them before the creation of the world.

Presbyterians/Presbyterianism. The Presbyterians believed that the church comprised the whole body of believers within a presbytery (a collection of parishes within a limited geographical area) ruled by elders (or presbyters), not by bishops. The power to rule was held not by the people but by the elders and other officeholders. Technically, there were few actual Presbyterians in seventeenth-century England. The label was applied to moderate Puritans whose preference was to see the Church of England reformed from within (see **reformation**). Baxter was a leading figure among these Presbyterians who wanted to belong within the church, not distance themselves from it.

Protectorate. The constitutional arrangement known as the Protectorate was established in December 1653 and vested supreme legislative authority in both Parliament and the "single person" of the Lord Protector. The first Lord Protector was Oliver Cromwell; when he died in September 1658, his son Richard was nominated to take his place. The Protectorate ended in May 1659 with Richard's forced retirement. Owen would have disliked the development of something that looked suspiciously like a monarchy; Baxter disliked Oliver Cromwell himself, but he appreciated the freedom to experiment under his rule and enthusiastically welcomed his son Richard Cromwell.

Protestant. A Protestant is someone who stands within a tradition stemming from the sixteenth-century Reformation. The label is also used to describe the theology of the Reformation. It derives from a "protestation" offered by the German Lutherans following their condemnation at the Diet of Speyer in 1529.

Puritans/Puritanism. A style of belief and piety that sought to "purify" the Church of England from all vestiges of its Roman Catholic past by returning to a way of life and worship indicated in the pages of the New Testament. Puritans were marked out by their elevation of the Scriptures as the sole authority in matters of faith and worship, by their careful observance of the Sabbath, by their scrupulous use of time, and by their desire to reform sin in society. In general, Puritans were the English embodiment of the convictions of the Swiss Reformation and Reformed theology.

Reformation. A variegated sixteenth-century movement spearheaded by Martin Luther and others who challenged the belief and worship of the Roman Catholic Church. These Reformers argued that the supreme authority in matters of faith and worship lay not in the pope or in church councils but in the Bible alone. Five catchwords mark out the central convictions of the Reformers: salvation by grace alone, through faith alone, on the basis of Christ's work alone, in accord with the Scriptures alone, to the glory of God alone. Yet the way they put those convictions into practice differed from country to country. Both Owen and Baxter sought to extend the Reformation in England.

reformation. The word *reformation* (with a lowercase *r*) refers to the effort to reform both the Church of England and English society (sometimes called the "reformation of manners") in line with the convictions of the Protestant Reformation. Generally, this involved trying to clear the church of any remaining taint of Roman Catholicism or any merely human innovations while also establishing the pure model of church worship and government laid out in the Scriptures. Baxter and Owen were both heavily invested in the aim of reformation.

Reformed theology. While this label might imply the theology of the Reformation in general, it encompasses the theology of the Swiss Reformation in particular. *The Reformed* is the name given to the Swiss Reformers, as distinct from *the Lutherans* of the German Reformation. The main distinctives of Reformed theology are a much more rigorous application of the notion of *Scripture alone*, so that church worship included only what the Bible explicitly permitted and approved, and an inclination to see the bread and wine of the sacraments as either only emblems or as elements in which Christ is spiritually present for our spiritual nourishment, while the Lutherans professed the "real presence" of Christ in the elements. While the German Reformation had an early influence in England, Reformed theology came to dominate during the sixteenth century. For all their differences, both Baxter and Owen saw themselves as working within the tradition of Reformed theology.

regicide. The regicide refers to the execution of King Charles I on January 30, 1649, for what were seen as his crimes during the English Civil War, thus initiating the Interregnum.

Restoration. In May 1660 Parliament brought the Interregnum to an end by voting to restore the "ancient constitution" formed around the monarchy, the House of Lords, and the House of Commons. England reverted to the constitutional settings in place when the English Civil War broke out in 1642. The bishops were also restored to their former place in the Church of England, and before long, most Puritans were ejected from any place of ministry within the church (see **Nonconformists/ Nonconformity**).

Scripture sufficiency. This term captures the essence of Baxter's adamant conviction that the only firm foundation for unity among Christians was the only text everyone could agree on: the Scriptures. Drafting a confession, especially one that went beyond the words of Scripture to introduce terminology that was merely human in origin, could only provoke disagreement and division. Owen favored such confessions and worried that Baxter's minimalist approach encouraged heretics such as the Socinians.

Socinians/Socinianism. A style of doctrine that denied many of the central doctrines of orthodox Christianity such as the Trinity and the deity of Christ. Socinianism was presented as a highly rational faith, one that saw those central doctrines as later human inventions overlaid on an otherwise simple scriptural account. It takes its name from the Italian theologian Faustus Socinus. In England Socinianism was deployed as a broad label against a range of different thinkers. Owen was correct to see the emergence of Socinianism in mid-seventeenth-century England as a serious threat to Trinitarian orthodoxy.

strict imputation. Baxter's term for what he felt was a key plank in antinomian theology, that when Christ died on the cross, he did so quite literally in the place of every individual member of the elect, and he made a payment for their sins that was the precise equivalent of their sins. So Christ took on their sin, and his righteousness was imputed to them. On this basis, antinomians argued that God does not see sin in any of the elect.

toleration. Early modern Europe held to the conviction that there was only one truth and that it would invite God's judgment if a nation was divided on what that was. Thus, uniformity of belief and practice in religious matters was of critical importance. Toleration opened up conceptual space for some ideas to be tolerated—not agreed with but tolerated. The question of which ideas could be tolerated and which could not was highly contested. Both Owen and Baxter supported toleration in the sense that neither felt that Christian belief was the proper focus of state coercion, though they were unwilling to extend toleration to Roman Catholics or atheists. See also **fundamentals, heretics/heresy,** and **orthodox/orthodoxy.**

Worcestershire Association. The Worcestershire Association was Baxter's idea, designed to bring about a working unity among his fellow ministers in Worcestershire. They agreed on a common method of pastoral care that involved meeting with those in the congregation at least annually, and they met monthly to encourage each other and to discuss difficult cases of church discipline. Similar associations sprang up in other counties, giving rise to what is known as the "association movement." Baxter was not the sole generator of the movement, but he was its principal sponsor and promoter. He believed this practice was the best way to bring about church unity on a national scale.

Further Reading

IF YOU ARE INTERESTED in reading further on Richard Baxter, John Owen, and the Puritans, here is a quick guide of some recommended sources. For the full publication details of each work I mention, see the select bibliography at the end of this section.

Let us start with the Puritans. If you would like a brief overview, you cannot beat a small book by Francis Bremer whose title says it all, *Puritanism: A Very Short Introduction*. For a much longer and deeper analysis, David Hall's book *The Puritans* expertly examines the Puritans in England, Scotland, and North America. If you are interested in a quick guide to seventeenth-century British history in general, try John Morrill's *Stuart Britain: A Very Short Introduction*.

Crawford Gribben has written the very best scholarly biography of John Owen: *John Owen and English Puritanism: Experiences of Defeat*. If you would prefer a shorter book that has much more of a Christian audience in mind, I recommend Gribben's *An Introduction to John Owen* or Matthew Barrett and Michael Haykin's *Owen on the Christian Life*.

We are long overdue for a new biography of Richard Baxter. The most recent, by Geoffrey Nuttall, was published in 1965.

For a lovely account of Baxter that presents him in a totally different light from the one in this book, see Vance Salisbury's *Good Mister Baxter*. Once again, the title says it all, and if you would like some reassurance about Baxter's many positive qualities, this is the book for you.

If you are interested to read some of what Baxter wrote, you might consider the modernized abridgments of his two classic works, *The Reformed Pastor* and *The Saints' Everlasting Rest*. For Owen, you might try the modernized version of his devotional classic *Communion with God*. All three books are published by Crossway.

As I explain in the introduction, this book is a shorter and more accessible version of my earlier book titled *John Owen, Richard Baxter, and the Formation of Nonconformity*. If you are interested in reading the full story or searching for further supporting evidence, here is how the chapters in this book line up with the chapters in that book:

When Christians Disagree	*Formation of Nonconformity*
chapter 2	chapter 1
chapter 3	chapter 4
chapter 4	chapter 2
chapter 5	chapters 3 and 7
chapter 6	chapters 5 and 6
chapter 7	chapters 8 and 9

My first book, *Fear and Polemic in Seventeenth-Century England: Richard Baxter and Antinomianism*, also has a chapter on personality that parallels chapter 3 of this book, and it engages fully with

Baxter's response to antinomianism presented in chapter 4 of this book. In that chapter, I speculate on the motivations behind the respective theologies of Baxter and Owen. These ideas are the focus of my chapter in *The Oxford Handbook of Calvin and Calvinism* and my article in the *Southern Baptist Journal of Theology*.

Select Bibliography

Barrett, Matthew, and Michael A. G. Haykin. *Owen on the Christian Life: Living for the Glory of God in Christ*. Theologians on the Christian Life. Wheaton, IL: Crossway, 2015.

Baxter, Richard. *The Reformed Pastor*. Updated and abridged by Tim Cooper. Wheaton, IL: Crossway, 2021.

Baxter, Richard. *The Saints' Everlasting Rest*. Updated and abridged by Tim Cooper. Wheaton, IL: Crossway, 2022.

Bremer, Francis J. *Puritanism: A Very Short Introduction*. Very Short Introductions 212. Oxford: Oxford University Press, 2009.

Cooper, Tim. "Calvinism among Seventeenth-Century English Puritans." In *The Oxford Handbook of Calvin and Calvinism*, edited by Bruce Gordon and Carl R. Trueman, 325–38. Oxford: Oxford University Press, 2021.

Cooper, Tim. *Fear and Polemic in Seventeenth-Century England: Richard Baxter and Antinomianism*. Aldershot, UK: Ashgate, 2001.

Cooper, Tim. "John Owen, Richard Baxter, and the Battle for Calvin in Later-Seventeenth-Century England." *Southern Baptist Journal of Theology* 20, no. 4 (2016): 63–78.

Cooper, Tim. *John Owen, Richard Baxter, and the Formation of Nonconformity*. Farnham, UK: Ashgate, 2011.

Gribben, Crawford. *An Introduction to John Owen: A Christian Vision for Every Stage of Life*. Wheaton, IL: Crossway, 2020.

Gribben, Crawford. *John Owen and English Puritanism: Experiences of Defeat*. Oxford Studies in Historical Theology. New York: Oxford University Press, 2016.

Hall, David D. *The Puritans: A Transatlantic History*. Princeton, NJ: Princeton University Press, 2019.

Morrill, John. *Stuart Britain: A Very Short Introduction*. Very Short Introductions 21. Oxford: Oxford University Press, 2000.

Nuttall, Geoffrey F. *Richard Baxter*. London: Thomas Nelson and Sons, 1965.

Owen, John. *Communion with the Triune God*. Edited by Kelly M. Kapic and Justin Taylor. Wheaton, IL: Crossway, 2007.

Salisbury, Vance. *Good Mister Baxter: Sketches of Effective, Gospel-Centered Leadership from the Life of Richard Baxter*. Nevada City, CA: Piety Hill, 2015.

General Index

Scripture Index

Also Available from Tim Cooper

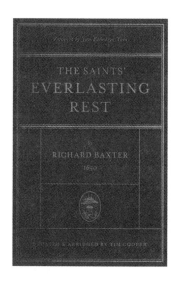

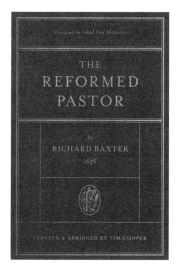

For more information, visit **crossway.org**.